LITERACY DEVEL[...]

ROLE PLAY

1 Reading Strategies and Development of Concepts of Print
- In the context of Modelled, Shared and Guided Reading and Writing:
  - clearly identify the purpose for reading
  - read and enjoy the text
  - demonstrate match between spoken word and printed word
  - discuss difference between print and pictures in context
  - focus on relationship between written and spoken language
  - use the pictures to gain additional information and to support the meaning derived from the text
  - use the rhythm and rhyme of language to predict the text
  - demonstrate that print is organised from top to bottom of a page and from left to right along a line
  - discuss title, cover, author, illustrator and contents page
  - model reading behaviours, including turning pages

2 Comprehension Strategies
- Engage children in Modelled, Shared and Guided Reading sessions, using simple before, during and after reading activities
- Discuss the characters in a story, the decisions they make and the actions they take
- Talk about the structure of stories and non-fiction texts. Show how understanding of structure helps comprehension
- Give children many opportunities to re-tell fiction and non-fiction texts both orally and through pictures

3 Reader Response
- Help children talk about texts, make judgements and begin to substantiate them with reference to the text
- Use the context of stories and informational texts to explore underlying values, relating these to everyday life
- Listen carefully to children's opinions, accepting difference and helping them explore the consequences of their thinking
- Help children understand that there is more than one resolution to a problem in a story. Provide opportunities to create alternative endings to stories having considered the impact of alternative decisions and actions

4 Accessing Information
- Show children how information can be gained from:
  - a range of sources such as books, newspapers, videos, audio-tapes, CD-Rom, posters, magazines
  - specific features in a text such as a simple diagram, picture or photograph
  - locating a specific portion of a book by using an index or contents page

EXPERIMENTAL

1 Reading Strategies
- Model and explain reading strateg[...] such as re-reading, reading on, self-monitoring and self-reflection in context
- Teach children to use reading strategies through activities such as oral cloze
- Provide opportunities for children to read aloud material that is predictable, familiar and contains natural repetition
- Consolidate and extend understandings of print through modelling, sharing and reflection activities

2 Comprehension Strategies
- Continue to provide opportunities for children to re-tell and discuss texts
- Continue to teach children fundamental reading strategies through the use of activities before, during and after reading
- Discuss main idea(s) of a text, drawing out literal and inferential meanings
- Help children relate text to own experience

3 Reader Response
- Encourage sharing and justification of opinions and feelings about characters, events and information
- Encourage and value diversity of opinion
- Comment on stereotyping of gender, age, role and perception of character
- Encourage children to participate in discussion and drama to develop the ability to identify with characters. Help them devise alternative consequences and story lines that would flow from an alternative decision made by a character
- Talk about authors and illustrators and how they draw on their own experience and perceptions

4 Accessing Information
- Provide children with opportunities to select reading materials relating to special interest or class topics
- Demonstrate how information on a topic can be found in a variety of sources and show how to access it appropriately
- Continue to model the use of title, cover, illustrations, diagrams, contents page and index

[...]

1 [...]ie[...]
[...]ow
monitoring and c[...]
re-reading, knowl[...]
understanding of [...]
and maintain me[...]
- Teach children to [...]
and graphophoni[...]
reading
- Provide opportuni[...]
aloud for a purpo[...]
- Teach children to [...]
portions of text fo[...]
Guided Reading s[...]
- Read aloud to chi[...]
fluency and expre[...]

2 Comprehension St[...]
- Help children ider[...]
key words after Sh[...]
Independent Read[...]
- Teach children a c[...]
through the integr[...]
monitoring and a[...]

3 Reader Response
- Demonstrate how [...]
are substantiated [...]
relevant parts of t[...]
- Discuss an author[...]
relation to childre[...]
- Discuss stereotypi[...]
facts, characters o[...]
in a particular wa[...]
has on the reader [...]

4 Accessing Informa[...]
- Assist children to [...]
informational nee[...]
appropriate sourc[...]
- Help children dev[...]
reading strategies [...]
scanning simple t[...]
purposes
- Model the use of c[...]
such as graphic o[...]
pyramids, flow ch[...]

ENTAL CONTINUUM

d and write from a
ave a sense of sentence,
with one or two elements
punctuation. Reading is
he focus is on accuracy.
be segmented into a series
nent when spelling, eg

and reading accuracy. This

urpose
line by line reading when
liar text
l expression
n reading unfamiliar text

s
short, simple, familiar texts
e-tell major content
pretive strategies to

comprehend and uses a
itoring and adjusting

tanding that all texts are
no are expressing their

reading materials from a

n from a range of sources
o at unfamiliar texts and
nd enjoyment when

nt detail in 'dawn to dusk'

amiliar text forms
xt some of the purposes of
ping list as memory aid

ing & Writing
tionship between sentence
e conjunctions eg *and,*

tructures and may vary
hen writing
punctuation in context
tters
riting

which are recognised when
ent contexts
racy of recognition of the
words
of word identification
nowledge of the topic;
nar; sounding out and
and simple letter patterns

inning letters and

rds drawn from language
literature, media and oral
d others
esents all substantial
thout regard for
g patterns eg *kaj (cage), tabl*
)
pellings for certain sounds
ulated rules eg *becoz*

individual handwriting

ng may deteriorate when
ands of writing

TRANSITIONAL

Transitional readers and writers are beginning to integrate reading and writing strategies. They read and write a range of text forms, but their writing may be characterized by rigid adherence to known formats. Their writing is becoming more conventional. They are beginning to monitor their comprehension, and adjust their reading strategies appropriately. They are beginning to use visual and meaning-based strategies for word identification and spelling.

TEXT LEVEL – Reading

1 ♦ Is able to discuss purpose for reading
♦ Is becoming efficient in using most of the following strategies when reading: makes and substantiates predictions; self-corrects; re-reads to clarify meaning; reads on; slows down and sub-vocalises when encountering difficult text; substitutes familiar words for unknown words; uses knowledge of print conventions

2 ♦ Can re-tell and discuss own interpretation of a range of texts with familiar concepts, providing information relating to plot and characterisation in fiction or to main ideas and supporting detail in non-fiction text
♦ Is aware of failure to comprehend and begins to use a range of monitoring and adjusting strategies

3 ♦ Recognises that characters can be stereotyped in a text and can discuss how this could be changed

4 ♦ Selects appropriate material from a range and adjusts reading strategies for different texts and different purposes eg *skims to gain a general idea and scans for a key word*

5 ♦ Is self motivated to read for a range of purposes, showing a marked preference for a particular author and genre

TEXT LEVEL – Writing

6 ♦ Attempts to orient the reader
♦ Attempts simple planning, eg *uses known framework or procedure*

7 ♦ Writes a range of text forms including stories, reports, procedures and expositions for appropriate purposes, but does not fully control these forms

SENTENCE LEVEL – Reading & Writing

8 ♦ Is becoming aware of the sentence patterns signalled by a range of conjunctions eg *therefore, however*
♦ Begins to use knowledge of common punctuation marks to enhance phrasing, intonation, and comprehension

9 ♦ Is beginning to write expanded sentences eg *understands and uses a small range of conjunctions and sometimes understands and uses subordinate phrases and clauses*

10 ♦ Punctuates simple sentences correctly

11 ♦ When directed uses proof-reading guide or checklist to edit own work

WORD LEVEL – Reading

12 ♦ Has an increasing bank of sight words including some difficult and subject-specific words, eg *science, topography, environment, diameter, latitude*

13 ♦ Is becoming efficient in the use of word identification strategies: graphophonics; common letter patterns; known parts of words; syllabification with word segmentation; grammar and syllabification; and knowledge of meaning eg *when encountering homonyms*

WORD LEVEL – Writing

14 ♦ Is beginning to select vocabulary appropriate to text form

15 ♦ Represents all vowel and consonant sounds in a word by placing a vowel in every syllable
♦ Is beginning to use visual strategies such as knowledge of common letter patterns and critical features of words

16 ♦ Is aware of the importance and quality of handwriting
♦ Controls basic formations and joins
♦ Is aware that quality of handwriting is not maintained when focus is on other factors

CONVENTIONAL

Conventional readers and writers have developed a multi-strategy approach to reading and writing a diverse range of texts. Their degree of control over structure, comprehension, vocabulary, punctuation and spelling varies according to the complexity of the task. Their use of language features may be contrived. They are becoming competent and independent but not sophisticated readers and writers.

TEXT LEVEL – Reading

1 ♦ Can explain purpose for reading
♦ Uses a range of strategies automatically to monitor and maintain meaning: makes and substantiates predictions; self-corrects; re-reads; reads on; slows down and sub-vocalises (when encountering difficult text); uses knowledge of context, print conventions and signal words

2 ♦ Reads and comprehends text that is abstract and removed from personal experience
♦ Makes inferences based on implicit information drawn from a text and can provide justification for those inferences by returning purposefully to the text
♦ Uses a wide range of monitoring and adjusting strategies to aid comprehension and is able to consciously select, use and discuss these strategies
♦ With support can discuss an alternative reading of a text and suggest why a text may be interpreted differently by different readers

3 ♦ Makes critical comparisons between texts

4 ♦ Applies some research skills effectively by using knowledge of informational needs, library organisation, text organisation, and relevant information sources

5 ♦ Discusses and recommends books, sharing opinions and enjoyment

TEXT LEVEL – Writing

6 ♦ Identifies likely audiences and adjusts writing to achieve impact
♦ Competently uses familiar processes to plan, draft and execute writing

7 ♦ Selects text forms to suit purpose and audience, demonstrating control over most essential elements

SENTENCE LEVEL – Reading & Writing

8 ♦ Uses knowledge of a growing range of signal words and phrases to identify relationships within sentences

9 ♦ Groups sentences into paragraphs
♦ Writes simple, compound and complex sentences

10 ♦ Interprets most punctuation marks correctly
♦ Uses most common punctuation marks correctly

11 ♦ Uses proof-reading guide or checklist to edit writing

WORD LEVEL – Reading

12 ♦ Reads known words automatically
♦ Can identify and explain words that enhance meaning in a text, including jargon, figurative language and technical words

13 ♦ Applies knowledge and uses word identification strategies appropriately and automatically when encountering an unknown word eg *graphophonics; common letter patterns; morphographs; word segmentation; grammar; and knowledge of meaning when encountering homonyms*

WORD LEVEL – Writing

14 ♦ Has accumulated a large bank of known sight words and is using more sophisticated language, albeit in a contrived way

15 ♦ Is aware of the many patterns and rules that are characteristic of the English language, and uses this knowledge in a multi-strategy approach to spelling

16 ♦ Has individual and fluent handwriting
♦ Is aware of the need to adapt handwritng according to audience and purpose
♦ Experiments with artistic or unusual scripts and computer-generated graphics

ROLE PLAY

Role play readers and writers are becoming aware of the relationship between written and spoken language. They display reading-like behaviours as they reconstruct stories and information based on their own experiences. They experiment with marks on paper as they emulate adult writing. Their 'writing' is not readable by others, as understanding of sound-symbol relationships have yet to develop.

TEXT LEVEL – Reading
1 ♦ Focuses on the meaning of a story or other text listened to or 'read'
  ♦ Demonstrates an awareness that writing and drawing are different eg *"Mummy reads the black bits"*
  ♦ Demonstrates an awareness that print says something but is not sure of the connection between print and speech
  ♦ Shows beginning awareness of directionality eg *points to where the text begins*
  ♦ Displays reading-like behaviour eg *holding the book the right way up, turning the pages appropriately, looking at words and pictures, using pictures to construct ideas*
  ♦ Uses pictorial and visual cues when 'reading' i.e. *talks about an advertisement or picture in a magazine or book, relating it to own knowledge and experience*
2 ♦ Re-tells familiar stories and information which have been listened to and viewed, focusing on meaning
3 ♦ Makes links to own experience when listening to or 'reading' books eg *points to illustration, saying "My dad doesn't do the washing!"*
4 ♦ Selects favourite books from a range eg *chooses a book, saying, "I want the Three Little Pigs"*
5 ♦ Displays curiosity about print and expresses enjoyment by joining in orally and responding when listening to familiar stories

TEXT LEVEL – Writing
6 ♦ May assign a message to own symbols
7 ♦ May state purpose for own 'writing' eg *"This is my shopping list"*

SENTENCE LEVEL – Reading & Writing
8 ♦ Uses sentence-like structures when 'reading'
9 ♦ 'Writes' sentence-like scribble or strings of simulated letters

WORD LEVEL – Reading
12 ♦ Recognises significant environmental print
13 ♦ Recognises own name, or part of it, in print
  ♦ May recognise familiar environmental print using context, location, shape of setting, accompanying logograph
  ♦ Recognises some letters of the alphabet

WORD LEVEL – Writing
14 ♦ Attempts to write own name
15 ♦ May use scribble, known letters and approximations of letters
16 ♦ Experiments with handwriting and pencil grip
  ♦ Enjoys tracing, copying and 'writing' for fun
  ♦ Conveys meaning through drawing which may be described in a dictated text

KEY	
1	Reading Strategies (Concepts of Print for Role Play)
2	Comprehension Strategies
3	Reader Response
4	Accessing Information
5	Attitude
6	Writing Strategies
7	Forms of text
8	Sentence Structure–Reading
9	Sentence Structure–Writing
10	Punctuation
11	Editing/Proof Reading
12	Sight Vocab and Vocab Enrichment
13	Strategies for Word Identification
14	Vocab Extension–Writing
15	Spelling
16	Handwriting

EXPERIMENTAL

Experimental readers and writers know what a word is and that letters represent sounds in reading and writing. They write simple sentence-like structures using the most obvious sounds of a word and the sounds of letter names when writing eg *DK-decay, PPL-people, KV-cave.* They use pictures, knowledge of the text and initial letters to help them read. They are focused on understanding and conveying the meaning of the text, rather than reading words accurately.

TEXT LEVEL – Reading
1 ♦ Reading is focused on expressing the meaning of a story, rather than on reading words accurately
  ♦ Matches some spoken words with written words when reading a book or environmental print
  ♦ May read simple, familiar, highly predictable texts with repetitive vocabulary, and supportive illustrations eg *Brown bear, brown bear...*
  ♦ Demonstrates understanding of concepts of print eg *uses left to right, top to bottom orientation of print*
  ♦ Demonstrates understanding that print contains a message and that written language conveys meaning
2 ♦ Uses prior knowledge of context and personal experience to comprehend eg *uses memory of a text to match spoken with written words*
3 ♦ Expresses opinion, favourable or otherwise about stories, but may not always be able to justify opinions
4 ♦ Identifies the subject matter of a text through the use of titles and illustrations
5 ♦ Chooses books to read and enjoys re-reading favourite stories

TEXT LEVEL – Writing
6 ♦ Assumes that a reader shares the context so may not give sufficient background information eg *may tell 'who' but not 'when'*
  ♦ Demonstrates one-to-one correspondence between written and spoken words
7 ♦ Attempts familiar forms of writing eg *lists, letters, recounts, stories, messages*

SENTENCE LEVEL – Reading & Writing
8 ♦ Reads back own sentence-like structures
  ♦ Reads familiar sentences with meaning but not always accurately
9 ♦ Writes simple speech-like sentences, eg *"I brt mi bik"*
10 ♦ Understands and experiments with significant punctuation in context eg *full stops, capital letters*

WORD LEVEL – Reading
12 ♦ Recognises personally significant words in context
13 ♦ Knows letters of the alphabet and can relate these to personally significant sounds. Begins to use onset/rime
  ♦ Begins to use knowledge of initial letters and related sounds, grammar and pictorial cues to predict significant words in text

WORD LEVEL – Writing
14 ♦ Uses a small bank of known sight words
15 ♦ Represents a whole word with one, two or three letters, using mainly consonants
  ♦ Relies heavily on the sounds most obvious to him or her eg *DN – down, WT – went, BAB – baby*
16 ♦ Attempts to formulate letters accurately
  ♦ Develops established pencil grip
  ♦ May reverse letters and may use upper and lower case letters indiscriminately
  ♦ Is confident that text and drawing are complementary and mutually supportive

EARLY

Early readers and writers r
personal perspective. They
but may only be able to de
at a time eg spelling but n
often word centred because
They know that a word car
of sounds and may over-se
theay-they, umpiyer-umpire.

TEXT LEVEL – Reading
1 ♦ Focuses on decoding
  may lead to:
  – a loss of sense of
  – word by word and
    reading an unfam
  – limited fluency ar
  – sub-vocalising wh
    silently
  – repeated re-readin
2 ♦ Is beginning to read
  confidently and can
  ♦ Uses literal and inte
  understand text
  ♦ Is aware of failure to
  limited range of mo
  strategies
3 ♦ Demonstrates under
  written by authors v
  own ideas
4 ♦ With help:
  – selects appropriat
    range of text form
  – gathers informati
5 ♦ Is willing to have a
  displays confidence
  reading

TEXT LEVEL – Writing
6 ♦ May include irrelevo
  recounts
7 ♦ Uses small range of
  ♦ Can explain in cont
  using writing eg *sho*

SENTENCE LEVEL – Read
8 ♦ Understands the rela
  parts joined by simp
  then, but
9 ♦ Uses basic sentence s
  sentence beginings v
10 ♦ Attempts to use som
  eg *full stops, capital l*
11 ♦ Sometimes corrects v

WORD LEVEL – Reading
12 ♦ Has a bank of words
  encountered in differ
  ♦ Is developing immed
  most frequently used
13 ♦ Uses some knowledg
  strategies including
  pictorial cues; gramn
  blending; onset/rime
  eg *ing*
  ♦ Relies heavily on beg
  sounding out

WORD LEVEL – Writing
14 ♦ Experiments with wo
  experience activities,
  language of peers ar
15 ♦ Sounds out and repr
  sounds in a word, wi
  conventional spellin
  (table), birgla (burglar
  ♦ Develops particular s
  often using self-form
  (because), woz (was)
16 ♦ Begins to develop an
  style
  ♦ Quality of handwriti
  focusing on new den

NUUM – Major Teaching Emphases

eaders use self-
rection, reading-on,
lge of the topic and
unctuation to make
ning
se semantic, syntactic
knowledge when

ies for children to read
e, eg *Readers' Theatre*
eturn to appropriate
substantiation in
ssions
lren daily, modelling
sion

ategies
tify central ideas and
ared, Guided and
ng
omprehension process
ation of awareness,
justing strategies

opinions about texts
by returning to
e text
s perspective in
's experience
g, questioning why
events are presented
y and the impact this

tion
dentify their
ls and select
s of information
lop appropriate
such as skimming and
xts for different

rganisational tools
tlines, mind-maps,
rts

TRANSITIONAL

1 Reading Strategies
- Model and explicitly teach a range of strategies such as self-reflection, self-monitoring, self-correction, reading-on, re-reading, knowledge of the topic, knowledge of the text form, linking prior knowledge to the text, making and substantiating predictions using print conventions and signal words
- Ensure that children read and talk about a range of texts for a variety of purposes, applying appropriate reading strategies for each
- Provide opportunities for children to read aloud expressively, eg *to younger children, in Readers' Theatre, auditioning for parts in a play, in choral reading and in Guided Reading sessions*

2 Comprehension Strategies
- Teach children to trace the development of an idea or theme through a text
- Teach children to monitor their comprehension through self-questioning before, during and after reading
- Teach children to substantiate responses to a text by returning to literal information in the text and identifying instances where inferences can legitimately be made. Help them relate findings to information from other texts and the media
- Teach children to substantiate literal, inferential and evaluative understandings from separated sections of text
- Model and discuss the conscious use of comprehension strategies in context

3 Reader Response
- Teach children to make critical comparisons with other texts
- Create a climate which fosters critical thinking. Alert children to the world view presented by an author
- Discuss how texts are written for different audiences. Stress that authors are real people with their own ideas and opinions and these are expressed in their books
- Use simple partisan texts to try and identify an author's values
- Discuss how readers may react differently to texts depending on their backgrounds and experience of life

4 Accessing Information
- Teach children to identify their informational needs; locate possible sources of information; select and extract relevant information using a jointly constructed framework; evaluate own work; and present information appropriately
- Model simple conventions of referencing

CONVENTIONAL

1 Reading Strategies
- Encourage children to reflect on how they integrate and adapt their reading strategies, eg *re-reading, slowing down, pointing, sub-vocalising and self-correcting, when reading a difficult or unfamiliar text*
- Talk about the use of different reading styles for different purposes
- Teach children to select and use relevant aspects of prior knowledge suitable for each text, eg *personal experience, topic knowledge, knowledge of text structure*
- Provide opportunities for children to read aloud on formal occasions

2 Comprehension Strategies
- Help children to identify their reading difficulties and learn how to select and use appropriate strategies
- Demonstrate how the same text and illustration can have layers of meaning
- Discuss the use of figurative language, eg *simile, metaphor, personification*
- Focus on literal, inferential and evaluative levels of comprehension with an emphasis on monitoring and substantiation within and beyond the text

3 Reader Response
- Help children understand that readers interpret texts in different ways and that texts can have many meanings
- Discuss the influence of culture, language and community experiences on writers' constructions and readers' interpretations of texts
- Teach children to interrogate a text from relevant standpoints, eg *point of view, character relationships, cultural influence*

4 Accessing Information
- Teach children to evaluate the effectiveness of their research skills, i.e.
  - analysing topics or questions
  - generating self-questions
  - selecting appropriate texts
  - summarising and taking notes
  - using self-selected organisational tools and frameworks
  - constructing reports
  - compiling bibliographies
- Ensure that children use and list appropriate references to support their writing

ROLE PLAY	EXPERIMENTAL	EARLY

ROLE PLAY

12 Sight Vocabulary and Vocabulary Enrichment
- Emphasise commonly used words in the environment, classroom and books. Use these words in games and draw attention to their use in Shared and Guided Reading and Modelled and Shared Writing sessions
- Talk about new vocabulary and use it in a range of contexts

13 Strategies for Word Identification
- Foster phonemic awareness through activities and games involving
  - the identification, segmentation and blending of sounds
  - the recognition, matching and generation of rhymes
- Use personal names to introduce sound/letter relationships and syllabification in play and activities
- Use play and song to teach the alphabet letter names
- Display and use an alphabet frieze
- Construct a class alphabet using children's names. Add other words appropriately, as they are taught
- Draw attention to the relationship between sounds and letters, fostering graphophonic awareness
- Link letters of the alphabet with matching sounds in context
- Use rhyme, rhythm and repetition in texts and games to heighten awareness of relationships between print and sound

14 Vocabulary Extension – Writing
- Talk about interesting words and encourage children to use them in speech and writing

15 Spelling
- Provide models of correctly written words in written responses to children's 'writing'

16 Handwriting
- Teach pencil grip in context

EXPERIMENTAL

11 Editing and Proof Reading
Teaching is designed to familiarise children with a process they will practise later
- Informally model how an author makes changes to text to enhance meaning
- Model simple corrections. Do not expect them to follow suit at this stage

12 Sight Vocabulary and Vocabulary Enrichment
- Introduce simple word recognition activities in context, praising children who recognise a word in a range of contexts
- With the children, build up a bank of interesting and evocative words

13 Strategies for Word Identification
- Continue to work with the class alphabet chart, adding words with the same initial letters
- Teach children to segment words into syllables
- Teach onset and rime through activities and games, stemming from familiar words eg 'I Spy'
- Continue to teach children to use contextual knowledge, patterns of language (syntax), initial letters, blending, onset and rime, sounding out, pictures and sight words to identify words when reading
- Talk about letters and words in context, pointing out distinctive features
- Help children segment words into individual sounds
- Help children represent sounds heard in words with letters written in the order they are heard

14 Vocabulary Extension – Writing
- Frequently refer to and model the use of words from class word banks and classroom print
- Enrich vocabulary through activities such as string writing

15 Spelling
Continue to develop and use all word identification strategies as above
- Model the use of class spelling charts, adding words with similar blends and medial vowels
- Teach children to use word banks, personal dictionaries and familiar books as spelling resources

16 Handwriting
- Teach pencil grip
- Help children understand starting points and direction when formulating letters

EARLY

11 Editing and Proof
- Model the use of simple editing
- Once children are jointly construct o beginning proof r

12 Sight Vocabulary Enrichment
- Extend basic sight involving childrer games and activit
- Enrich vocabulary as string writing
- Teach subject spec measure – maths, – literature

13 Strategies for Wor
- Teach a range of strategies, such as in big words, usin sentences to deter needed to make s to identify words
- Help children use common letter sec rime, word compc sounding out and to identify words

14 Vocabulary Extens
- Build personal an focusing on them words etc

15 Spelling
- Teach children to features of words: different sounds, s different letters
- Continue to build to provide a syste and a record of re
- Teach children so strategies, eg Look

16 Handwriting
- Ensure good penc poor habits are n
- Foster clear and f
- Help children inte through handwrit

NUUM – Major Teaching Emphases

TRANSITIONAL	CONVENTIONAL

Reading
roof reading and

writing confidently,
simple guide for
ading

nd Vocabulary

vocabulary by
in word recognition
es
through activities such

fic words in context eg
xygen – science, limerick

l Identification
ord identification
identifying little words
the structure of
nine the type of word
nse, eg *He k...... a goal*

visual patterns,
uences, onset and
nents, syllables,
knowledge of meaning

ion – Writing
l class word banks
words, descriptive

dentify differentiating
etters representing
punds represented by

a class spelling chart
natic view of spelling
ent learning
ne word-learning
Cover, Say, Write, Check

grip. Make sure that
t allowed to develop
ient handwriting
nalise spelling
ng

TRANSITIONAL

11 Editing and Proof Reading
- Model the use of proof reading, editing and simple revisions
- Jointly refine and expand proof reading guide to include editing strategies and elements of text revision
- Ensure that children proof read their work after it has been edited

12 Sight Vocabulary and Vocabulary Enrichment
- Discuss and teach subject specific vocabulary and ensure that children can immediately recognise most common words
- Continue to enrich children's vocabularies by searching for evocative and interesting words, and jointly constructing an Interesting Word Chart
- Discuss use of figurative language and technical terms

13 Strategies for Word Identification
- Teach word identification strategies i.e. *use of context, graphophonic knowledge, sounding out, blending, letter and word patterns, sight words, syllabification, segmentation, root words, word components, prefixes, suffixes and morphographs*

14 Vocabulary Extension – Writing
- Continue to add interesting, subject specific and evocative words to word banks

15 Spelling
- Continue to teach visual patterns. Problem solve, construct and chart a list of spelling rules. Make hypotheses and prove/disprove/amend as evidence accumulates
- Introduce Spelling Journal. Teach word-learning strategies. Help children to make up and use mnemonics

16 Handwriting
- Encourage children to take pride in their handwriting
- Encourage experimentation with a range of scripts
- Explore computer graphics and presentation

CONVENTIONAL

11 Editing and Proof Reading
- Model the use of proof reading, editing and revising
- Discuss and evaluate the effective use of the planning, monitoring and revising processes of writing
- Jointly construct an effective Editing Guide
- Editors' marks could be researched and incorporated

12 Sight Vocabulary and Vocabulary Enrichment
- Analyse texts, examining the use of specific words and how they enhance meaning and convey subtle meaning

13 Strategies for Word Identification
- Reflect on the use of a range of word identification strategies, eg *word derivation, roots, components*

14 Vocabulary Extension – Writing
- Continue to extend knowledge of subject specific vocabulary. Extend knowledge of roots, prefixes and suffixes

15 Spelling
- Continue to use Spelling Journal
- Explore word derivation
- Focus on meaning as a guide to spelling
- Teach complex visual patterns such as *scious,* and irregular spellings such as *forfeit* and *quay*
- Continue to problem-solve rules, recording on a jointly constructed chart
- Encourage memory aids such as mnemonics

16 Handwriting
- Help children modify writing to suit purpose, eg *developing speed-writing techniques for note taking*
- Foster development of individual styles, but ensure that focus on decorative script does not disrupt clarity and legibility
- Encourage further exploration and use of computer graphics and modes of presentation

Key Stage Two
PRIMARY 4–7

How to assess, plan and teach

Information Texts 2

Information Texts, Key Stage 2

was written by

Ross Bindon

Senior Consultant

Education Department of Western Australia

Contents

SECTION **3**

BRINGING IT ALL TOGETHER

GLOSSARY

BIBLIOGRAPHY

UK BIBLIOGRAPHY

ACKNOWLEDGEMENTS

TITLES IN THIS SERIES

FIRST STEPS PROFESSIONAL DEVELOPMENT

INTRODUCTION

From the moment a child rises in the morning and reads the back of a cereal packet through half-opened eyes, to the news report provided at the close of an evening's television viewing, daily life is rich with the comprehension and composition of information texts. There are instructions to follow, messages to be written and information to be found in a variety of contexts. It is critical that pupils develop the skills to access, comprehend and generate information to meet their needs.

Not all factual information, however, is to be found in explanations and arguments, reports and recounts. Many narratives may be based on fact, and have as their purpose to inform or to persuade.

This book deals with information texts specifically because of what these texts have in common. Information texts generally are written to describe, inform, explain, instruct or persuade. Although the text form, text structure and language features chosen to achieve each purpose may differ, the strategies we use to make sense of these texts are often similar. For example, whether a person is reading a newspaper report or an advertisement, it is likely that the reader is assessing what they already know about the subject of each.

For pupils surrounded by the richness of story in their early years, the comprehension of fictional material is natural and reassuring. The story of Cinderella told in their home language is similar to the one they saw on video at a carer's house, and the one the teacher read at Nursery. To act out the tale there is a well-established understanding that characters and a setting are needed, and that events will unfold, leading to a climax, and a resolution. Over time pupils will come to learn that the story form will vary greatly, but many of these 'signposts to comprehension' will remain as recognisable features.

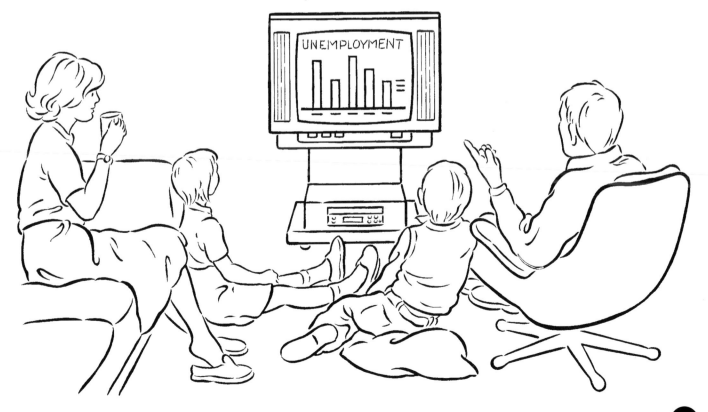

Non-fiction material is different. Some children do not bring to school a wealth of experience with information texts. Those children who do may not have their experience recognised in the school setting. Although the ways of sharing information in many cultures is changing, factual material has not had the same place in early literacy learning as narrative material. Often information has been passed from generation to generation within a storytelling form. For many pupils the structure and language features of non-fiction materials are less familiar than the narrative form. The signposts are not as easy to recognise. In the place of a setting, characters, problems and resolutions, the pupil must learn to recognise definitions, topic sentences, sub-headings and summaries.

Learning to compose information texts will be very helpful to pupils who need to recognise such signposts. They will come to see a how a variety of text forms are structured to achieve particular purposes. However, the demands on readers and writers of non-fiction are greater than this alone. Pupils will need explicit teaching to become aware that the tone of authority in information books is open to dispute. They will recognise that all text carries with it a set of values that inevitably reflect the culture and the views of the author. In its simplest form this may be recognition that the cereal manufacturers promote their cereal with healthy, muscular characters to help the reader associate their consumption with this body type. At a more sophisticated level there may be an awareness that a history text has left out a key event or figure, providing a biased interpretation of the period. Only as inquiring readers and writers will pupils become aware of the need to consult a number of up-to-date, authoritative sources before drawing conclusions from non-fiction material. This will be critical for a generation of pupils who will do much of their reading from sources like television and the Internet.

How to Use this Book

The knowledge, skills and strategies required for reading and writing information texts effectively are inseparable. Knowledge of text structure and language features grasped by the pupil in writing lessons is used an aid to comprehension in reading lessons. Similarly the teaching of ways to find the main idea in reading has enhanced pupils' ability to combine related information into paragraphs in writing. It is for the purpose of clarity of framework and ease of organisation that this book has been divided into text types and strategies that are designed primarily for writing, and strategies that are predominantly for reading. In both sections references to reading and writing are made, and many more are inferred.

It is recommended that readers use the *First Steps* Literacy Developmental Continuum to assess their pupils' control of the writing process and text types, and their ability to comprehend non-fiction materials. By examining the pattern of Indicators teachers will be able to select a broad direction. For example, pupils with a limited sense of purpose and audience in writing will benefit from the strategies described in this book that focus on the writing process. Pupils who are displaying a control of the writing process but lack confidence in writing a variety of text types need instruction taken from the text types section of this book. It is suggested that – at least initially – teachers focus on one process (e.g. writing for a purpose and audience), one text type (e.g. explanation) or one skill (reading to find the main idea) at any one time to consolidate learning.

All strategies are designed as part of a cohesive sequence of work, and most are best used in the context of modelled, shared and guided reading. Where a particular text type is the teaching focus, strategies follow the description of each text type. Where the focus is a more generic one, like comprehending information texts, these strategies have been categorised as *before, during* and *after* to clarify their role in facilitating comprehension. Teachers familiar with the text types and strategies outlined in this book will be able blend the objectives of a Literacy Hour by using a strategy to explore a text type. For example, having introduced pupils to the structure of a report earlier in the week, the teacher might use a pyramid strategy (see page 93) to establish the main idea of a number of paragraphs. Pupils will conclude that the main idea of each paragraph corresponds with the framework of a report and learning will be consolidated. Of course, this interweaving of objectives is heavily dependent on the preceding demonstrations and sharing of report writing and pyramiding being successful.

The success of a unit of work or sequence of lessons will also rely on the usefulness of the text. A list of criteria for useful materials is given overleaf. Some strategies described in the latter half of this book are text-dependant. This may mean that the text must have sub-headings or distinct topic sentences to enable the strategy to work. Teachers who develop an 'eye' for useful texts are able to take advantage of non-fiction features such as glossaries, diagrams and headings in their lessons.

A pyramid strategy

Information texts	Text feature
• are rarely read from cover to cover	• so a contents page and index make the text accessible
	• so headings and sub-headings direct the reader
• are about facts	• so photographs and diagrams are more prevalent than illustrations
	• so opinions and emotive language are rare
• usually involve the use of subject-specific language	• so a glossary is often included
	• so context clues are often supplied
• have a structure based on ideas rather than plot	• so a framework is sometimes used to organise the text
	• so paragraphs usually group information relating to one idea
	• so paragraphs often begin with a topic sentence to signal what the paragraph is about

Choosing Effective Information Texts

Choosing effective information texts is critical to the success of reading and writing programmes. By collecting, analysing and displaying a wide range of effective information texts, pupils build knowledge about the structure and language of factual material. They develop a sense of why authors write about information and for whom they write. This is essential knowledge that underpins many of the skills and strategies explained in this book.

An effective information text is one which makes the reading process as easy as possible for the reader. By considering the characteristics of information texts, the ways in which they accommodate the reader can be listed.

It is not necessary, and indeed may not be possible, for texts to be chosen on the basis of their resemblance to the text type frameworks suggested in this book. Professional authors often use their knowledge of a number of text types to write a text. To repeatedly write to a framework would be limiting and counter-productive. Furthermore, it is important that pupils see the range of ways in which a text type can be written.

The content of the texts will be a factor in their success. Probably more so than fiction texts, information texts need to be interesting and motivating. Texts that address objectives in other curriculum areas allow the teacher to plan for an integrated unit of work in which reading and writing is done for a real purpose.

Yet another criterion is readability. Where possible, pupils need to be matched to texts appropriate to their reading ability. As a rough guide, if pupils are being troubled by more than one in every ten words, the text is too difficult.

Where teachers have a limited selection of information texts, pupils can be supported with scaffolded reading tasks and intense pre-reading activities that concentrate on building background knowledge.

Supporting the Reading-Writing Connection

Reading and writing are mutually supportive ways of functioning in a literate world. When readers and writers share meaning through print and other media, they draw upon similar stores of knowledge, think critically and creatively to shape and interpret ideas, and wrestle with the written word. Readers and writers battle a common foe – the void created by time and distance. In face-to-face oral communication feedback, gesture and body language are useful and timely ways of clarifying meaning. The speaker usually has opportunities to correct misconceptions, reaffirm statements and emphasise key points. The listener can probe and question in search of meaning. However, written communication robs readers and writers of these tools, forcing them to use a different range of strategies to cope with being prisoners of the printed word.

Although readers and writers have much in common, they retain the unique characteristics of their perspectives. The reader is primarily fixed on comprehending: making sense of a text by superimposing personal background and experience on a text. The writer's main concern is composing: creating a text that makes sense to a wide range of readers. Yet the roles are rarely exclusive. Effective readers and writers are forever switching roles in their minds. The reader may be thinking, 'Why has the author chosen to introduce this information at this point? What effect will this have on my understanding of the topic?' The reader is making attempts to see the world through the author's eyes. The writer, on the other hand, is thinking, 'If I introduce this information at this point, will the reader link it to the main idea? How can I help the reader understand the main points in this chapter?' The writer is making attempts to see the world through the reader's eyes. By mapping the processes of reading and writing, the mirror images can be made more explicit. As teachers become familiar with reading-writing connections, they can help children use them to their advantage.

To a degree the processes of reading and writing are mirror images. The following table attempts to map the nature of these cyclic processes while accommodating the styles and idiosyncrasies of individual readers and writers. The thinking processes of awareness, monitoring and adjusting are ongoing, and provide the reader or writer with direction and confirmation.

Awarness – Monitoring – Adjusting

The reading process	The writing process
Before reading	**Before writing**
The social trigger A 'social trigger', such as a need for information, pleasure or curiosity, creates a reason to read. Triggers might include using a VCR, exploring a world of romance or wanting to know if a film star is pregnant. The reader is asking, 'Why am I reading?'	**The social trigger** A 'social trigger', such as a desire to reflect, persuade, inform or entertain, creates a reason to write. Triggers could be clarifying personal thoughts, being a dissatisfied customer or letting someone know that you'll be late home. The writer is asking, 'Why am I writing?'
Activating background knowledge The reader brings to the text expectations about its purpose, its medium, its form, its author and its content. A schema, or mental map, based on previous experiences and knowledge, is activated to maximise comprehension. The reader is asking, 'What do I know about this medium, this form, this author, this topic?'	**Activating background knowledge** The writer thinks about the writing – its purpose, its medium, its form, its audience and its content. These elements are interdependent, and the writer begins to balance their impact by mentally rehearsing the shape the text might take. The writer is asking, 'What do I know about this medium, this form, this audience, this topic?'
Surveying the text The reader uses initial impressions of the text layout to confirm or reject initial predictions about purpose, medium, form, author and content. The reader is asking, 'What do I know about the structure and language features of this form of text? What signposts do I recognise?'	**Preparing the text** The writer selects a medium and a text form appropriate to the purpose, content, context and audience of the writing. The structure of the form is used to make planning notes or conduct research if it is necessary. The writer is asking, 'How can I use the structure and language features of this form of text to achieve my purpose? What signposts could I construct for the reader?'

During reading – simultaneous processes	During writing – simultaneous processes
Comprehending meaning The reader begins a cyclic, recursive process of predicting, sampling, confirming or rejecting at the Word, Sentence and Text Level. The reader is asking, 'What does this mean?'	**Composing meaning** The writer begins a cyclic, recursive process of drafting, revising and editing at the Word, Sentence and Text Level. The writer is asking, 'Is this what I mean?'
Managing the mechanics The reader uses graphophonic, syntactic and semantic cues to decode the text. The reader is asking, 'Does this make sense?'	**Managing the mechanics** The writer is using spelling, grammar and punctuation to encode the text. The writer is asking, 'Is this making sense?'
Reading beyond the text The reader is questioning the view of the world presented by the author. The reader is asking, 'How am I being positioned by the author?'	**Creating meanings beyond the text** The writer is (intentionally or unintentionally) creating a view of the world that complements the purpose of the text. The writer is asking, 'How can I position the reader?'
Taking personal meaning from the text The reader is being changed by the text. Information is being used to reframe ideas, reflect on attitudes or act upon. The reader is asking, 'How will I feel or act differently as a result of reading this text?'	**Making personal meanings in the text** The writer is attempting to change the reader by adding to and revising their store of knowledge, shape their attitudes or move them to action. The writer is asking, 'How can I involve the reader personally in the text?'

After reading	After writing
	Publishing The writer presents the text in a finished format appropriate to the standards of the context, purpose, form and audience. The writer is asking, 'Does this finished format support the meaning I am trying to make?'
Reflecting and sharing The reader reflects on the personal impact of the text and (possibly) shares some thoughts with others. A judgement about the worth of the text may be made, a response crafted (a review), or a decision made about further reading choices pertaining to that genre, author or topic. The reader considers whether the social trigger has been satisfied, and makes a decision about future reading choices. The reader is asking, 'Did I get the information, pleasure or satisfaction I wanted from this text? Do I need or want to read another text of the same subject or genre? Did my reading trigger a desire to read a different text?'	**Reflecting and sharing** The writer reflects on the process, often having afterthoughts and doubts. The writer seeks out feedback on the text. A judgement about the worth of the text may be made, a response crafted (a review), or a decision made about future writing pertaining to that genre, audience or topic. The writer considers whether the social trigger has been satisfied, and makes a decision about future writing choices. The writer is asking, 'Did the reader get my message? Is there a need for a sequel? Did my writing trigger a desire to write a different text?'

(Adapted from Freebody in *Prevention of Reading Failure*, Watson and Badenhop, Ashton Scholastic, Gosford, 1992.)

TEXT TYPES

The text types addressed in this book are generally considered to be those most often required in Key Stage 2. Each text type includes an explanation of its typical structure and language features. Examples of the text type and suggestions about contexts and strategies for teaching are made. It must be remembered that the text type frameworks are simply a starting point for pupils learning to write to achieve a purpose. The framework for persuasive texts, for example, does not reflect the structure or features of a dramatic tabloid advertisement or the bluntness of a political slogan scrawled on a wall, yet both could be called persuasive texts. The intention has been to share frameworks that are widely accepted, and features that commonly appear in texts of that type. In introducing pupils to particular text types, teachers can draw widely from texts to show how a range of texts achieve a similar purpose. A narrower focus is necessary, however, when pupils are required to identify, collect and analyse text types in preparation for writing (*We have collected a wide range of persuasive texts, but the one I'd like to teach you to write is this one…*).

Instructions, Directions and Procedures

Instructional texts direct the reader to carry out a series of actions or steps to accomplish something. As a result, instructions often also describe, inform and explain, but the main purpose is to direct.

Purpose and Types

Instructions can be oral, written or in diagrammatic form. Sometimes they can be combinations of two or all three of these modes. This book deals with written and diagrammatic instructions.

Instructions play an important role in our everyday life and are used in many contexts. When people follow a recipe, assemble a toy or operate a machine, they follow instructions.

The following texts are types of instructions:

– directions

– procedures

– recipes.

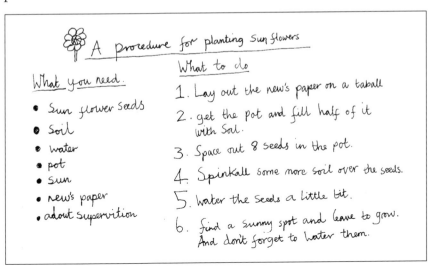

Instructions for growing sunflowers by Kerry (Year 4)

Applications Across the Curriculum

All areas of the curriculum involve activities and processes that benefit from use of instructions. Many of these instructional situations will be oral, involving one pupil explaining to a partner or a small group the steps necessary to complete a task. However, some instructions need to be written down because they are too lengthy or complex to be remembered. Some instructional texts will be encountered in day-to-day reading as pupils engage in tasks beyond their personal experience.

As part of the ongoing learning processes of reflecting, representing and reporting, the writing of instructions (representing) helps pupils clarify their thoughts and reshape their ideas.

The following curriculum activities could involve the use of written instructions.

English	How to research a topic
Geography	How to use an atlas to locate a city
Maths	How to find the area of a circle
Health Education	How to pick up things correctly
Science	How to replicate an experiment
Physical Education	How to warm up before sport
Art	How to weave a cane basket

How to Pick Up Things Correctly

By following the instructions provided you will be able to pick up items safely, without hurting your back.

1   Bend at the knees, keeping your back straight.

2   Pick up the article that is in front of you.

3   Straighten up, letting your legs do the work.

If you remember to do this you will have a strong and healthy back.

Text Organisation	Text framework headings may vary in different contexts, but the overall structure is the same. For example, a machinery manual may include safety warnings before the method, or software installation instructions may include a troubleshooting guide to trace problems in implementation.

An instructional text generally has four components. Each stage has a separate and distinct function.

- The **goal or aim** states what is to be done. It may describe a situation that has arisen and requires instructions to be resolved. (*If the computer shows the message* system error 1, *follow these steps...*) A goal could just as easily be a destination to be reached, a model to be built or a pest to be eradicated. Sometimes, as is often the case with recipes, the goal or aim is encompassed in the title. It is assumed that the reader is aware that a recipe explains how to prepare a food therefore the name of the dish alone is sufficient to clarify the purpose of following the instructions.

- **Materials or requirements** needed to complete the task are typically listed in order of use. The materials may be tools, instruments or utensils, ingredients, parts or data.

- A series of steps makes up the **method**. The steps may be numbered, abbreviated or accompanied by diagrams, depending on the purpose of the instructions. Occasionally the method is presented as connected sentences or paragraphs. Headings and sub-headings are sometimes used to organise long lists of steps.

- The final and optional element of an instructional text is the **evaluation**. The evaluation is sometimes omitted because the writer assumes that the reader can assess whether the instructions have been followed correctly. This is often the case where the goal is explicit, and to repeat it is seen as unnecessary. The success of many instructional texts, such as directions to a destination, is obvious. In others a photo or illustration of an assembled model or a cooked meal provides sufficient information to assess the instructions.

Language Features	Instructions are based on activities. They arise from the need for a writer to convey to a reader how to do something. Generally, the activity or operation is a physical act like baiting a hook or knitting a scarf, but sometimes more abstract topics like 'Coping with Children' or 'Accepting Criticism' are written in an instructional way.

Many instructional texts in daily life are oral. The context of the situation, the body language and the possible physical guidance of the instructor, an assessment of the knowledge of the listener and the opportunity to confirm and clarify instructions are all factors that enhance the communication. However, it is not practical for all instructions to be provided orally. Furniture manufacturers can't always afford to have telephone helplines to assist customers in the assembly of their goods. Listeners can't always remember the directions to a specific location hours later when they are stuck in traffic. Time and distance are often barriers to oral instructions.

Several other factors will influence the language features of an instructional text. The relationship between the giver and receiver of instructions is pivotal. Instructions given by a teacher to a pupil will differ from those given by a pupil to a teacher because there are social expectations attached to those roles. When a parent shows and tells a child how to tie her shoelaces, there is a great deal of assumed knowledge. If the same parent is required to give navigational directions to a complete stranger over the phone, the language used will change. The goodwill between the two parties may also affect the detail provided and the manner in which it is delivered. Similarly the subject of the instructions and the relationship between the giver and receiver of instructions will affect the formality of the language used in the procedure.

The importance of reading or writing instructions lies in the clarity of the instruction provided. Unlike the oral procedure, context clues are minimal, and little can be left to chance. In the operation of machinery or the mixing of chemical substances, for example, the consequences of ambiguous instructions could be dire. The writer of an instructional text must cater for readers who have a range of background knowledge, yet still use vocabulary that is specific enough to be accurate. It is necessary that the language of instructions be:

- brief, so it can be translated into action easily

- clear and specific, so there is no doubt about the intended message

- systematic and/or sequential, so actions are carried out in a productive order.

Instructions generally have:

- verbs to describe actions, e.g. hold, bake, twist, wedge

- the reader referred to as 'you' or not referred to at all

- linking words to do with time, e.g. first, then, when

- simple present tense, e.g. passes, grinds, locks

- detailed, subject-specific, factual description of materials, e.g. the shortest screw, 4 ounces of flour, the external drive

- detailed information about how, where and when.

(Adapted from Derewianka, B. 1990, *Exploring How Texts Work*)

The following chart demonstrates the typical organisation and language features of an instructional text.

Goal	Making Marbled Card
What is the aim of the instuctions?	Marbling is the art of colouring or staining an object so it looks like marble. It is easy to do and results in unique and beautiful patterns that can be used to decorate cards, book covers and boxes. This set of instructions explains how to make marbled card.
Materials	• Small leftover amounts or sample pots (50ml) of enamel or oil-based paint (at least three different colours) • Turpentine • A dish at least 5cm deep and wide enough for the sheets of card to lie flat • Sheets of card, clean, white paper and scrap paper • Small paint brushes • Water • Rubber gloves • A stirring tool. An old fork or clean stick would be fine.
Steps	1 Put on the rubber gloves. 2 Pour water into the dish until it is 1cm from the rim. 3 Add small blobs of paint to the surface of the water using one paint brush for each colour. 4 Swirl the blobs gently with your stirring tool. 5 Wait for 10 minutes. 6 Slowly lower a piece of card into the water until it is just underneath the surface, taking care to keep the card flat. 7 Lift the card gently, keeping it flat. 8 Place the sheet, pattern facing down, on to a sheet of clean white paper. 9 Place a sheet of scrap paper on top to soak up any extra water or paint. 10 Peel back the scrap paper, and then the card to reveal the marble print.
Evaluation	The marble print should be colourful and distinct. Several prints can be made from the print bath before more paint blobs will need to be added.

A Problem-Solving Approach to Teaching Instructional Writing

A problem-solving approach to teaching the writing of instructions is an effective way to help Early, Transitional and Conventional writers to improve their written procedures.

Use shared reading sessions to show children different types of instructional texts, their purposes and who might use them. The following texts can be used as a starting point for children to discuss instructions and to devise a framework that can be refined over time. These texts were written by eight-year-olds before a class discussion about the techniques of effective recipe-writing. The pupils were asked to write how they had made pikelets at school so they could take the instructions home and try out the recipe again. Some had little experience of cooking and using recipe books, while others had participated in cooking both at home and at school. Their writing reflects their experiences.

Interspersed with the sample texts are the discussion comments of another class of eight-year-olds, and how the teacher paraphrased the discussion to write statements that would form the basis of a framework and guidelines for the writing of a procedure.

Example 1

Instructions	Pupils said:	Teacher wrote:
Pikelets • flour • bicarbonate of soda • sugar • egg • sour milk • butter Sift the first two things into a bowl. Put the other things in. You have to melt the butter first. Mix it all up. Cook the pikelets in a hot frying pan. Eat them hot or cold with butter.	Example 1 is set out clearly but there are no amounts in it and the method is jumbled.	Steps not in order. No exact quantities.

Example 2

Instructions	Pupils said:	Teacher wrote:
We made some pikelets Today in Room 7 we made pikelets. We all had a turn at sifting the flour and the bicarbonate of soda. I put the sugar in, Angela put the egg in and Isnin put the milk in. We all stirred it but Isnin knocked over the bowl and some of the stuff spilt out. I cleaned up the mess. When it was mixed we poured in some melted butter and mixed it up. We cooked the pikelets and ate them. They were yummy!	I think Example 2 isn't a recipe because it just tells about the day. It doesn't even tell how much of each ingredient is needed. You shouldn't write about spilling stuff because that isn't anything to do with how to make pikelets.	No information about ingredients. Irrelevant information included.

Example 3

Pikelets Ingredients: 1 cup self-raising flour $\frac{1}{2}$ teaspoon bicarbonate of soda 2 tablespoons sugar 1 egg $\frac{1}{2}$ cup sour milk 60 grams butter **Method:** 1 Sift together flour and bicarbonate of soda. 2 Add egg, milk and sugar. 3 Mix. 4 Pour in melted butter. 5 Mix. 6 Place by spoonful into hot pan (160°C) 7 Cook until bubbling. 8 Turn to brown other side.	Example 3 is the best. It has a title. It lists the amount and the name of each ingredient. The instructions are short and clear, and it doesn't include unnecessary details. The instructions start with a thing to do, not with 'you' all the time.	Title tells what is to be made. Ingredients and amount are listed clearly. Instructions are in order and contain detailed information that helps the user. The steps begin with a verb, or doing word, not 'you'.

Example 4

Instructions	Pupils said:	Teacher wrote:
How to make pikelets Instructions: You have to get a cup of self-raising flour, $\frac{1}{2}$ teaspoon of bicarbonate of soda and sift them into a bowl. Then you have to put in one egg, 2 tablespoons of sugar and $\frac{1}{2}$ cup of sour milk, and stir the mixture up so it looks not lumpy. You have to melt the butter and mix it with the other stuff. You heat the electric frying pan and put a spoonful in each corner. When you have cooked the pikelets they taste great. I like to eat the mixture before it cooks.	Example 4 is hard to follow, although the information is all there. It says 'you' all the time. That isn't necessary because the reader knows it means him/her.	Information isn't easy to find. 'You' is not needed to start each step.

The pupils continued to work through the examples, making comparisons and comments which were noted by the teacher. The comments they made indicated that they already had ideas about how procedural texts should be constructed.

The teacher recorded her comments like this:

Effective instructions	Ineffective instructions
Title tells what is to be made. Ingredients and amount are listed clearly. Instructions are in order and contain detailed information that helps the user. The steps begin with a verb, or doing word, not 'you'.	Steps not in order. No exact quantities. No information about ingredients. Irrelevant information included. Information isn't easy to find. 'You' is not needed to start each step.

The children reviewed their information and constructed their 'Guidelines for Writing Instructions', which was represented as follows.

Guidelines for Writing Instructions

1 Begin with a title that tells what has to be done.
2 List exactly what ingredients or things are needed for the procedure.
3 Write the steps in order.
4 Begin each step with a verb.
5 Leave out unnecessary information and words like 'you'.

Planning Frameworks

The planning framework on page 23 encourages pupils to take notes and begin to write a draft with the framework of a procedure in mind. However, it is critical that pupils have a solid understanding of the framework and language features before they attempt to use these planning outlines. Pupils need the accumulated learning experiences described in Section 2 of this book if they are to benefit from planning frameworks.

Pupils need to know that planning frameworks are intended to make the organisation of a first draft of a procedure easier. Where frameworks are restrictive, adaptations can be discussed with the pupils and more appropriate outlines developed. Plans are a preliminary scaffold; as pupils' writing development progresses the plans will become redundant.

Instructions Plan

AIM/GOAL/TITLE:
What is to be done?

_____

REQUIREMENTS/MATERIALS/INGREDIENTS/TOOLS:
What is needed for this task?

- _____
- _____
- _____
- _____
- _____
- _____
- _____
- _____

METHOD:
What steps need to be followed?

1 _____
2 _____
3 _____
4 _____
5 _____
6 _____
7 _____
8 _____
9 _____
10 _____

EVALUATION/TESTING:
How does the reader know that the instructions have been successful?

_____
_____
_____
_____
_____
_____
_____
_____
_____

Assessment and Evaluation of Instructional Writing

The Indicators on the following page trace the development of instructional writing. Teachers may choose to use the Indicators to assess pupils' control of instructional writing.

Pupils will rarely display Indicators from only one Developmental Phase, so teachers will need to use professional judgement to determine the main Phase in which the children are working. Directions for the future teaching of instructional writing become evident by examining the next Phase of Development.

Often a pattern of achievement can be detected through the use of the sub-headings, *Purpose, Text Organisation and Content*, and *Language Features*. For example, a group of pupils may exhibit most of the Indicators under the sub-headings *Purpose* and *Text Organisation and Content* in the Consolidating Phase, but also exhibit Indicators under the sub-heading *Language Features* in the Beginning Phase. This would suggest that the pupils understand the framework of a set of instructions, but are unaware of the language specific to instructional writing.

Procedures

PROCEDURE INDICATORS

BEGINNING

Purpose:
The writer:
- discusses the use of simple procedures such as recipes

Text Organisation
- writes observation and comment or a recount

Goal
- briefly mentions goal, e.g. 'This is how you make a cake'

Materials
- mentions some materials

Method
- requires help to include all steps of procedure in correct sequence
- illustrates steps of procedure
- uses labels or captions for illustrations of procedure

Language Features
- uses language close to speech, e.g. 'The first thing you do is put an egg in.'
- links steps using 'and then'
- uses generalised 'you', e.g. 'you put some bananas in then you mash them'

DEVELOPING

Purpose:
The writer:
- discusses the purpose and advantage of written instructions

Text Organisation and Content
- uses a procedure framework

Goal
- states purpose or goal

Materials
- lists materials required

Method
- includes most of the necessary steps of procedure in sequence
- illustrates to support text

Language Features
- maintains simple present tense throughout
- uses linking words to signal time, e.g. *first, when, then, after*
- omits 'you' and starts sentences with a verb or adverb, e.g. *Stir, Add, Cut, Carefully glue*
- uses action verbs

CONSOLIDATING

Purpose:
The writer:
- can identify and describe a range of purposes for written procedures

Text Organisation and Content
- structures text using or adapting a procedure framework

Goal
- states goal precisely

Materials
- lists materials required, under a heading
- shows some evidence of appropriate layout

Method
- states method or instruction in correct sequence with adequate detail
- uses diagrams to support text

Language Features
- writes referring to classes of things (ingredients; equipment) as well as specific ones (the flour, the salt)
- refers to reader in general way (one/you) or does not mention the reader (turn the handle, add the water)
- maintains simple present tense throughout
- develops coherence through use of linking words such as *after, next, while, during, secondly, finally*
- uses subject-specific vocabulary
- includes some explanations to justify results

EXTENDING

Purpose:
The writer:
- demonstrates understanding of a large range of contexts where written procedures may be used to tell how to do or make something
- accurately interprets need of the audience by identifying and including relevant information in written procedures

Text Organisation and Content
- selects and uses an appropriate procedure framework for different contexts
- uses layout that is appropriate to the subject and topic

Goal
- states goal using precise terminology appropriate to the context and form

Materials
- clearly lists all materials and quantities required

Method
- writes explicit instructions for sequence of steps required to complete task
- includes detailed information on 'how', 'where' and 'when' each step is to be completed
- uses diagrams, photographs, illustrations to elaborate and support text where appropriate
- evaluates outcome (optional)

Language Features
- uses procedural order to provide text cohesion
- uses appropriate terminology
- uses linking words to do with time, e.g. *first, next, after ten minutes*
- guides reader accurately by use of precise adverbs or adjectives, e.g. *slowly unwind the larger spool, carefully cut a 10cm wide strip from the left side*
- uses simple present tense, e.g. *stir the mixture until it boils*
- refers to the reader in a general way or not at all, e.g. *'you mix', 'one mixes', or 'mix'*
- selects appropriate headings for stages of procedure according to context and purpose, e.g. Goal/Aim/Hypothesis, Utensils/Equipment/Ingredients.

(Adapted from Rivalland, J. and Raison, G. (1990) Education Department of Western Australia: Perth)

Newspaper Reports	Newspaper reports inform readers of an event or events. They are written to keep readers reading the newspaper and to attract new readers. In reporting events, newspaper reporters inevitably reflect a view of the world, sometimes in a deliberate attempt to appeal to a specific audience.
Purpose and Types	Newspaper reports are sometimes called news stories, news articles or news items. They have much in common with news reports on the television and on the radio.
Applications Across the Curriculum	Newspaper reports are a valuable source of current, relevant reading material for many curriculum areas. Consider how the following articles could be used to enrich lessons in curriculum areas.

Opportunities to write newspaper reports are created when pupils are involved in newsworthy events that can be reported to a defined audience. Excursions, notable visitors, unexpected happenings, sporting events, arts festivals and major personal achievements are all newsworthy. Classroom, school and local newspapers provide the medium for sharing this news with an interested community.

Pupils can also role-play the writing a newspaper report by transforming other forms into a newspaper report form. For example, having read a fairy tale like Goldilocks and the Three Bears, pupils can write a newspaper report, describing the major events. This activity places demands on a pupil's comprehension of the text, and his/her ability to reshape the events in newspaper report language.

| **Text Organisation** | A newspaper report generally has at least three components. Each stage has a separate and distinct function. Three further components are optional. |

- A **headline** is generally abbreviated, describing the essence of the report in the least possible number of words. It is often intended to capture the interest of the reader, so may be a pun or a play on words such as *Snappy Recapture for Escaped Alligator.*

- An optional component that sometimes follows the headline is the **by-line**. The by-line simply announces who wrote the report.

- The **lead or introduction** consists of one or two sentences packed with the essential elements of the report: who, what, when, where, why, how. It is brief, but encapsulates all the details necessary for a summary of the event or events.

- Further detail about the circumstances of the event and the people involved is provided in the **body** of the report.

- Sometimes **sources**, which are opinions from participants in the event, or any experts in the particular field of interest, are included in the text. Sources may be used early in the text (*A University Professor today declared that shaking hands a health risk…*), in the body of the text, or at the tail or end of the text.

- Another optional component is the **photograph and caption**.

| **Language Features** | Newspaper reports are based on recent, newsworthy events that may be local, national or international, and can range from around 50 words up to around 300 words. They are rarely simple recounts or narratives, yet elements of both those text forms are often apparent. What makes the newspaper report unique as a text form is the newspaper medium. Newspapers have to contain plenty of information for readers who usually have limited reading time. |

With so much varied information packed into a newspaper it is important that the headline or photograph attracts a reader's attention. Then, assuming the headline or photograph has been effective in luring the reader, the information must be immediate and easy to read. Lead paragraphs are loaded with vital information, but are carefully constructed to maintain the reader's attention and allow them to judge whether they would like to read on. Sentences are rarely excessively long or weighed down with unnecessary elaboration. There is also the possibility that a sub-editor may choose to cut or limit the length of the report to suit the space available, so the most important information must be included early in the text. If further detail is necessary, the report is accompanied by a feature article commenting on the major issues.

Newspaper reports appear to be authoritative to many readers. It would seem that reporters are simply describing events from a neutral or unbiased position. However, upon further examination, this is rarely the case.

Bias may be evident through:

- what is considered newsworthy
- how it is reported
- what is left out
- sources that are consulted
- the photograph and caption.

The language of a newspaper report may range between formal and informal, depending on the subject matter and the target audience for the newspaper. Newspaper reports generally contain:

- verbs to describe actions, e.g. struck, flooded, denied
- past tense, e.g. killed, chased, celebrated
- detailed information about who, what, when, where, why, how.

The following chart illustrates the organisation and language features typical of a newspaper report.

Headline What is the main idea of the newspaper report?	On the dog and bone
Lead Who? Where? When?	A London woman who lost a mobile phone called the number to hear it ringing inside her friend's dog.
Body What are the details?	Rachel Murray had left the phone under her Christmas tree as a surprise gift for her flatmate, but his bloodhound, Charlie, got to it first. After searching for three hours Ms Murray dialled the mobile phone number only to hear muffled ringing inside Charlie's stomach. She at first thought he was lying on the phone, but then realised where it was. A vet advised them to let nature take its course. A day later the phone emerged in perfect working order.
Source(s)	'We spent most of that night watching him every time he went to the loo. Suddenly it just came out – we couldn't stay cross for long,' Ms Murray said. The phone company said, 'It's amazing where you can get a signal on one of our phones.'

<table>
<tr><td>

A Problem-Solving Approach to Teaching Newspaper Report Writing

</td><td>

A problem-solving approach to teaching writing newspaper reports is an effective way to help writers improve their understanding of this text form.

Shared and guided reading sessions provide ideal contexts for the discussion of a variety of newspaper reports. The following examples can be used as a starting point for pupils to discuss newspaper reports and to devise a framework that can be refined over time. These texts were written by eight-year-olds before a class discussion about the techniques of effective newspaper report writing.

Interspersed with the sample texts are the discussion comments of another class of eight-year-olds, and how the teacher paraphrased the discussion to write statements that would form the basis of a framework and guidelines for the writing of newspaper reports.

</td></tr>
</table>

Example 1

Newspaper Report	Pupils said:	Teacher wrote:
Painting Sprayed Some men in a truck came to clean off the painting on the wall on Tuesday. They parked their truck next to Room 13, hopped out, opened up the back, pulled out a long hose with a pistol thing on the end, and started up an engine that made the pistol start spraying. It took quite a while for the painting to come off.	The heading is short, but it isn't really clear. Middle sentence is too long.	Headline is too short — unclear. Sentences must be easy to read.

Example 2

Newspaper Report	Pupils said:	Teacher wrote:
Vandalism Removed On Tuesday, 4th May, workers from a company called Cleaning Agents used heavy spraying equipment to clean graffiti from the wall outside Room 13. The two men involved arrived just after 10am and began spraying high pressure jets of special chemicals. It took almost 30 minutes to remove the vandalism. Our head teacher, Ms Evans, said it was disappointing that some of the money we had saved for new sporting equipment had to be spent on removing graffiti. She asked everyone who lived near the school to report any person loitering in the school grounds outside school hours.	It has lots of information. It uses good words like graffiti and chemicals. It has a comment from a person, which makes it more interesting.	Lots of information. Specific words. Includes a comment from someone involved.

Example 3

Newspaper Report	Pupils said:	Teacher wrote:
Vandals in Trouble On Tuesday the spray paint writing on our school was sprayed off. Men used big gun things to squirt stuff all over the wall. Ms Evans told me anyone caught vandalising the school would be reported to the police.	Not enough detail. Headline is not about the cleaning. The sentences don't sound like newspaper sentences.	Not enough specific detail. Headline doesn't sum up the report. Language too informal (first person rather than third person).

Example 4

Newspaper Report	Pupils said:	Teacher wrote:
Vandalism Has Been Cleaned Off Outside Room 13 The vandalism on the wall outside Mrs Copping's room has been cleaned off. People in a white truck came and sprayed it all off. I hope that whoever did it will get caught next time they vandalise someone else's property.	Headline is too long. The report doesn't have enough information. It has some information that is not needed: the description of the truck. It has a personal comment that is not needed.	Headline needs to be short. Not enough specific information. Too much irrelevant information. The writer's opinion is not necessary.

The pupils continued to work through the samples making comparisons and comments, which the teacher jotted down. The comments they made indicated that they already had ideas about how newspaper reports should be written.

The teacher recorded her comments like this:

Effective newspaper reports	Ineffective newspaper reports
Headline — short and clear. Lots of information. Specific details — who, where, what, when, how, why. Includes a comment from a person involved. Formal, newspaper language — no use of *I* or *me*.	Headline — long and not about the report. Not enough detail. Informal language. Irrelevant information included. Reporter's opinion included.

The children reviewed their information and constructed their 'Guidelines for Writing Newspaper Reports'. It was represented like this:

Guidelines for Writing Newspaper Reports

1   Begin with a headline that is short, but sums up the report.
2   Include information about *who, when, what, where, how* and *why*. Be specific.
3   Write in newspaper language. Don't use *I* or *me*.
4   Leave out your (the reporter's) opinions.

Planning Frameworks

The planning framework on page 32 encourages pupils to take notes and begin to write a draft with the framework of a newspaper report in mind. It is critical that pupils have a solid understanding of the text organisation and language features before they attempt to use planning frameworks. Pupils need the accumulated learning experiences described in Section 2 of this book before they can fully benefit from the use of planning frameworks.

Pupils need to know that planning frameworks are intended to make the organisation of a first draft of a newspaper report easier. Where the frameworks are restrictive, adaptations can be discussed by the pupils and more appropriate outlines developed.

Newspaper Report Plan

HEADLINE:
In the least number of words possible, what is the main idea of the report?

_____

LEAD SENTENCE(S):
What are the facts of this event: who, what, where, when, why, how?

_____
_____
_____
_____

BODY:
What supporting information can be included?

_____
_____
_____
_____
_____
_____
_____
_____
_____
_____
_____
_____
_____
_____

SOURCE(S):
Did a person involved in the event make a comment?
Did an expert in this field make a comment?

_____
_____
_____
_____
_____
_____

Assessment and Evaluation of Newspaper Report Writing

The Indicators on the following page trace the development of newspaper report writing. Teachers may choose to use the Indicators to assess pupils' control of newspaper report writing.

Pupils will rarely display Indicators from only one Developmental Phase, so teachers will need to use professional judgement to determine the main Phase in which the children are working. Directions for the future teaching of newspaper report writing become evident by examining the next Phase of Development.

Often a pattern of achievement can be detected through the use of the sub-headings, *Purpose, Text Organisation and Content*, and *Language Features*. For example, a group of pupils may exhibit most of the Indicators under the sub-headings *Purpose* and *Text Organisation and Content* in the Consolidating Phase, but also exhibit Indicators under the sub-heading, *Language Features*, in the Beginning Phase. This would suggest that the pupils understand the framework of a newspaper report, but are unaware of the language specific to newspaper report writing.

NEWS REPORT INDICATORS

BEGINNING

Purpose:
The writer:
- uses news reports to publicise a personal experience

Text Organisation and Content
- writes a recount with limited description
- sometimes sequences events

Headline
- writes a lengthy headline that only partially reflects the content of the report

Lead
- provides basic information about context, often assuming prior knowledge and excluding essential elements e.g. where or when

Body
- lists events in chronological order with little description

Sources
- makes little or no reference to sources

Language Features
- uses oral language structures
- often assumes prior knowledge of reader
- includes first person references

DEVELOPING

Purpose:
The writer:
- uses news reports to publicise a personal experience

Text Organisation and Content
- includes who, where and when in lead, and sequences events

Headline
- writes a headline that reflects the content of the report

Lead
- includes all the essential elements of a lead, i.e. who, where, when, what, why, often in a stilted sentence structure

Body
- sequences events, including some that have minimal relevance

Sources
- makes limited reference to sources

Language Features
- begins to use formal language structures e.g. In the playground today...
- provides adequate background detail
- writes in the third person
- usually maintains simple past tense

CONSOLIDATING

Purpose:
The writer:
- selects newsworthy events appropriate for reporting

Text Organisation and Content
- writes a concise, but informative lead, and supplies supporting detail in the body of the report

Headline
- writes an abbreviated headline that reflects the literal content of the report

Lead
- includes all essential elements of a lead in a fluent, sophisticated sentence structure

Body
- describes key events that underpin the lead

Sources
- uses at least one source to enhance the body of the report

Language Features
- uses the formal language typical of a newspaper report
- caters for a wide audience by explaining background and jargon where necessary
- writes consistently in the third person
- maintains simple past tense
- signals time by using a limited range of words as markers or linking words, e.g. Once the fight was over... The following day...

EXTENDING

Purpose:
The writer:
- is aware of own bias in selection of events and how they are reported

Text Organisation and Content
- writes a concise lead that lures the reader to comprehensive and cohesive supporting detail

Headline
- writes an abbreviated, snappy headline that attracts readers to the lead and body of the report and captures the essence of the report content

Lead
- uses a variety of sentence structures to include the essential elements of a lead, saving detail for the body of the report

Body
- selects, describes and where necessary elaborates upon key events that underpin the lead, and support the writer's perspective

Sources
- selects sources from more than one point of view

Language Features
- uses the formal language typical of a newspaper report, varying sentence structure and avoiding cliches to interest the reader
- caters for a wide audience by providing reference to previous relevant events, and by explaining background and jargon where necessary
- writes consistently in the third person
- maintains simple past tense or manipulates tense where appropriate
- signals time by using a wide range of words as markers or linking words, e.g Subsequently... As a result of the theft...

| **Persuasive Texts** |

| *Purpose and Types* |

The purpose of a persuasive text is to develop ideas and supporting details in order to present a logical argument from a particular point of view. Although the primary aim is to persuade the reader to agree with a writer's particular point of view or thesis, the author may also inform, explain and analyse issues and events.

The following texts are sometimes types of persuasive texts:

— essays

— advertisements

— critical reviews

— persuasive letters.

| *Applications Across the Curriculum* |

The reading and writing of persuasive texts is most critical to discussion and learning in those areas of the curriculum that focus on society, community and human endeavour. This does not preclude their use in subject areas like art and design and technology, but it will be the application of those disciplines in society that provides the basis for argument, rather than their subject content itself. Here are some examples of how teachers have used the power of argument in curriculum areas:

English	Should euthanasia be legal?
Geography	For or against proposed changes in the locality
History	For or against British involvement in WW2

| *Text Organisation* |

A formal written argument has three essential components. Each stage has a distinct function and may consist of more than one paragraph.

- Arguments generally begin with a statement of the basic position of the author and/or an overview of the topic or question. This is called the **thesis**.

- A **series of arguments** intended to support the thesis follows. Usually each argument occupies one paragraph, and provides evidence in the form of facts, statistics or examples to support the author's position.

- The **conclusion** of an argument is generally a brief summary of the series of arguments presented and a restatement of the thesis. Sometimes the conclusion can include a call to action (*So, in closing, it is critical that the person in the street accepts the responsibility for recycling rubbish on a regular basis…*).

| *Language Features* |

The key to the success of an argument rests in the tone of the text. Often the author must walk a fine line between the use of logic and reason, and the appeal of emotive language. The balance will be adjusted according to the audience and its relationship to the author. For example, one would expect a letter persuading a bank manager to loan money to be formal and based heavily on reason and logic. A flier protesting against the building of an industrial complex next to the school, and aimed at local residents, however, may include more emotive language.

Arguments generally have the following language features:

- words or phrases that connect the 'thread' of the argument, e.g. furthermore, on the other hand

- participants – these can be generic human, e.g. the homeless, Europeans or car owners, or abstract non-human, e.g. dislike, oppressed, dissatisfied

- timeless present tense (except where historic evidence is tendered)

- actions are frequently changed into things to make the argument sound more objective, e.g. '...the erosion of our liberties...' as opposed to 'our liberties are being eroded...'

- vocabulary can be technical, depending on the audience.

(Adapted from Derewianka, B. (1990) *Exploring How Texts Work*)

The following chart illustrates the organisation and language features typical of a persuasive text.

Thesis What is the author's position?	Using examinations to assess a pupil's ability to succeed in further training is unfair. To collect ongoing indications of a pupil's school performance would be a far more logical and accurate way of deciding whether access to further education should be given.
Arguments	Some pupils perform poorly in exam situations for a variety of reasons. It is human nature to have 'off' days. On such days two- or three-hour pen and paper assessments will not reflect a person's true ability. Even those who are having good days are being judged excessively on their reading and writing skills. Employers have made it clear that they require workers with excellent interpersonal skills, problem-solving skills and values like initiative and perseverance. Exams don't test those skills and qualities. To measure the skills and qualities that count, educators need to observe pupils over time. A pupil's ability to work at a consistent level and pace is most evident in an analysis of a portfolio of work or a series of marks collected from a wide range of learning situations. This sustained effort can not be accurately measured by an examination.
Summary	There are several reasons why examination scores should not be the deciding factor on what a pupil does next in his or her life – the fact that anyone can have a bad day; the fact that exams can't actually test what employers want in a worker; the fact that exams can't show how a pupil works over a sustained period of time. These are just a few of the reasons why exams should be replaced with results collected in a range of situations over a long period of time.

A Problem-Solving Approach to Teaching Persuasive Writing	A problem-solving approach to teaching persuasive writing is an effective way to help writers improve their understanding of this text type.

A problem-solving approach to teaching persuasive writing is an effective way to help writers improve their understanding of this text type.

Shared and guided reading sessions provide ideal contexts for the discussion of a variety of persuasive texts. The following texts can be used as a starting point for pupils to discuss persuasion and to devise a framework that can be refined over time. These texts were written by eight-year-olds before a class discussion about the techniques of effective persuasive writing.

Interspersed with the sample texts are the discussion comments of another class of eight-year-olds, and how the teacher paraphrased the discussion to write statements that would form the basis of a framework and guidelines for persuasive writing.

Example 1

Persuasive text	Pupils said:	Teacher wrote:
I think it should be banned because it is cruel. Foxes can be controlled by other methods like poisoning and trapping. My uncle has a farm and he said you don't see many foxes these days anyway. It's okay for people to go riding, but it's not necessary that they chase some poor animal.	Is unclear in the beginning. Has some good opinions, but sounds a bit personal.	Doesn't state position clearly. Good opinions. Sounds personal.

Example 2

Persuasive text	Pupils said:	Teacher wrote:
Fox hunting should be banned because an animal is being pursued for fun. It may be fun for the hunters but it is extremely cruel to the fox. We would not consider torturing any other animal in this way, so why is it done to foxes?	The first sentence introduces the topic clearly.	The introduction states the writer's position clearly.
	Each paragraph starts with a sentence that describes what it is about.	Each paragraph has a topic sentence.
	The words used make it sound like the author knows what they are talking about.	The writer uses specific vocabulary.
Foxes are no longer the pest they once were in some areas. If they were they could be eliminated by more humane methods like trapping. It is likely that more damage is being done to farms by hunters than by foxes.	The writer doesn't keep saying I think.	The writer states opinions as if they were facts.
	The paragraphs are sort of linked.	Repeated words and ideas link the paragraphs.
Hunters, apart from trampling the environment with their horses, spend their time arguing that fox hunting is a tradition. Many traditions, like burning witches at the stake have been abandoned because they make no sense. Fox hunting makes no sense.		
Fox hunting is cruel, unnecessary and makes no sense. It should be banned immediately.		

Example 3

Persuasive text	Pupils said:	Teacher wrote:
Fox hunting should not be allowed. Just because some people enjoy chasing an animal until it dies or is mauled to death, it doesn't mean it's right.

Foxes don't kill many things. Foxes are smaller than the hounds. Foxes have feelings like humans. Foxes don't have many places to live. | Has a good, strong introduction.

Has a list of opinions. Doesn't elaborate on any of them.

Has no conclusion or summary. | Introduction must include a strong statement of position.

Each argument should be explained.

Has no conclusion or summary. |

Example 4

Persuasive text	Pupils said:	Teacher wrote:
Fox hunting is stupid.

I saw fox hunting on telly once and it was stupid. All these people were wearing these funny clothes and blowing bugle things. I don't think I would enjoy fox hunting. | Lists opinions.

Has a personal tone.

Includes irrelevant information. | Has opinions — needs facts.

Has a personal tone.

Includes irrelevant information. |

The pupils continued to work through the samples making comparisons and comments, which the teacher jotted down. The teacher recorded her comments like this:

Effective persuasive text	Ineffective persuasive text
State position or thesis clearly in the opening paragraph. Not personal — no use of I or me. Opinions are supported and sound like facts. Paragraphs have topic sentences. Have specific vocabulary. Paragraphs are linked. Each argument is explained. Have a conclusion or summary. Include descriptive, relevant information.	Doesn't state position clearly. Personal language. Unsupported opinions. Paragraphs are poorly formed. Lack specific vocabulary. Paragraphs are not linked. Arguments lack elaboration. Includes irrelevant information.

The children reviewed their information and constructed their 'Guidelines for Writing Persuasive Texts'. It was represented as follows.

Guidelines for Writing Persuasive Texts

1 Make your position clear in the opening paragraph.
2 Explain each argument in detail.
3 Write in argument language. Don't use I or me.
4 Begin each paragraph with a topic sentence.
4 Link the paragraphs.
6 Use specific vocabulary.

Planning Frameworks

The planning framework on page 40 encourages pupils to take notes and begin to write a draft with the framework of a persuasive text in mind. It is critical that pupils have a solid understanding of the text organisation and language features before they attempt to use planning frameworks. Pupils need the accumulated learning experiences described in Section 2 of this book before they can fully benefit from the use of planning frameworks.

Pupils need to know that planning frameworks are intended to make the organisation of a first draft of a persuasive text easier. Where the frameworks are restrictive, adaptations can be discussed by the pupils and more appropriate outlines developed.

Persuasive Text Plan

THESIS:
What is the position of the author?
_____
_____
_____

ARGUMENTS:
Argument 1 _____
Supporting evidence _____
_____
_____
_____
_____
_____
_____

Argument 2 _____
Supporting evidence _____
_____
_____
_____
_____
_____

Argument 3 _____
Supporting evidence _____
_____
_____
_____
_____

SUMMARY/CONCLUSION:
What are the key points of the persuasive text?
What was the thesis?
_____
_____
_____
_____
_____
_____
_____
_____
_____
_____

Assessment and Evaluation of Persuasive Text Writing

The Indicators on the following page trace the development of persuasive text writing. Teachers may choose to use the Indicators to assess pupils' control of persuasive writing.

Pupils will rarely display Indicators from only one Developmental Phase, so teachers will need to use professional judgement to determine the main Phase in which the children are working. Directions for the future teaching of persuasive text writing become evident by examining the next Phase of Development.

Often a pattern of achievement can be detected through the use of the sub-headings, *Purpose, Text Organisation and Content*, and *Language Features*. For example, a group of pupils may exhibit most of the Indicators under the sub-headings *Purpose* and *Text Organisation and Content* in the Consolidating Phase, but also exhibit Indicators under the sub-heading, *Language Features*, in the Beginning Phase. This would suggest that the pupils understand the framework of a persuasive text, but are unaware of the language specific to it.

Expositions

PERSUASIVE TEXT INDICATORS

BEGINNING

Purpose:
The writer:
- discusses reasons for writing

Text Organisation and Content
- shows little evidence of organisation

Thesis
- writes an opening sentence that reveals personal position, e.g. 'I don't think they should chop down trees.'

Argument
- uses little or no justification for viewpoint

Reiteration or Conclusion
- writes a final statement that may not refer to position taken
- offers no conclusion

Language Features
- writes in language close to speech, e.g. "I reckon it's not fair…'
- writes from first person point of view

DEVELOPING

Purpose:
The writer:
- discusses reasons for writing

Text Organisation and Content
- attempts the use of an exposition framework

Thesis
- writes opening statement that reveals position to be taken in exposition
- expresses thesis subjectively, e.g. *I think…*

Argument
- includes arguments in an arbitrary manner without classifying or organising logically
- provides some supporting evidence

Reiteration or Conclusion
- concludes with a personal statement, e.g. 'Therefore I don't think it is fair because…'

Language Features
- uses imprecise adjectives or adverbs
- writes using personal viewpoint
- uses simple conjunctions, e.g. *and, then, but*
- writes using language close to speech

CONSOLIDATING

Purpose:
The writer:
- sees writing as a means to an end

Text Organisation and Content
- uses the organisational framework of an exposition
- presents information logically

Thesis
- writes an opening paragraph that provides context and uses generalisation to conceal subjective viewpoint
- attempts to provide some context for argument following

Argument
- provides adequate information in some planned or systematic way
- selects details loosely related to the topic
- attempts to generalise
- includes some personal judgements that lack supporting evidence

Reiteration or Conclusion
- attempts to summarise with a paragraph that substantiates the position adopted

Language Features
- uses an impersonal style
- develops coherence by use of additive conjunctions, such as *too, every, also* and adversative conjunctions, such as *however, although, on the other hand*

EXTENDING

Purpose:
The writer:
- uses writing to persuade others

Text Organisation and Content
- effectively organises relevant information using the framework of an exposition
- demonstrates understanding of the function of each stage of an exposition

Thesis
- writes an opening paragraph that consists of a thesis (or position) followed by a brief summary of the arguments to follow

Argument
- locates and uses relevant information
- provides relevant evidence to support assertions
- plans arguments logically
- generalises to authenticate the argument e.g. 'Vehicles pollute the air.'
- presents each paragraph to state a point and then elaborates
- establishes the relationship between part and whole by introducing and concluding each paragraph to lead from one point to the next

Reiteration or Conclusion
- writes a final paragraph that reiterates the main points with an evaluative conclusion

Language Features
- clearly defines words and selects the most effective words for the context
- maintains point of view
- uses complex logical structures to provide authenticity
- expresses actions as things (nominalisation) to make argument seem more objective, e.g. 'Pollution is caused by cars.'
- conceals personal bias through use of objective language, i.e. uses emotive words objectively, e.g. *concern*
- maintains consistency of tense (usually timeless present), e.g. 'Trucks are ruining…'
- uses a variety of verbs, often in passive voice, e.g. *It is believed… roads are ruined…*
- uses adversatives, e.g. *conversely*
- uses controlling words such as *to begin, similarly, finally*
- uses more complex conjunctions, such as *moreover, furthermore, in fact, for example*

(Adapted from Rivalland, J. and Raison, G. (1990) Education Department of Western Australia: Perth)

Explanations	The purpose of an explanation is to explain some phenomenon, that is, how things occur, or how things work.

Purpose and Types	Explanations broadly fall into two categories:

- those that explain how things work, e.g. how a vacuum cleaner works

- those that explain why things happen, e.g. why volcanoes erupt.

Many explanations are a combination of these two categories.

Applications Across the Curriculum	Explanations are used throughout the curriculum wherever objects and processes require explanation. The following are just a few examples of how explanations can be used.

Social Studies	The water cycle
Music	How a clarinet works
Health Education	How the ear works
Science	How electricity is generated

Text Organisation	An explanation generally has at least four components. Each stage has a separate and distinct function.

- Most explanations begin with a **statement** about, or a **definition** of, the phenomenon to be explained. The purpose of this paragraph is to orient the reader.

- This is sometimes followed by a description of **components** or **parts**, although this is optional.

- The heart of an explanation is the **operations** paragraph, which describes in explicit cause and effect terms how or why the phenomenon works.

- Another optional stage of the explanation is the description of the **application** of the phenomenon, which states when and where it works or is applied.

- The final and optional element of an explanation is the **evaluative summary**. The evaluative summary sometimes includes reference to any special features of the phenomenon.

Language Features	Explanations generally contain some or all of the following features:

- generalised non-human participants (the motor, volcanoes, currents)

- words indicating cause and effect relationships (if/then, so, as a consequence, since)

- mainly action verbs (falls, rises, changes)

- timeless present tense (are, happens, turns)

(Adapted from Derewianka, B. (1990) *Exploring How Texts Work*)

The following chart illustrates the organisation and language features typical of an explanation text.

| Definition
What is the object or phenomenon? | How a Kite Works
A kite is a flying object that is heavier than air. |
|---|---|
| Components or parts | A kite consists of a frame, a skin covering the frame and a long string that is held by the user. |
| Operations | A kite becomes airborne when the wind pressure between the kite and the ground lifts the structure into the air. The tilt of the plane surface of the kite causes a lesser air pressure to occur behind the kite's upper surface than the wind on the under-surface. |
| Applications | Kites have been used as signals, experimental instruments in atmospheric measurement and as play objects dating back many thousands of years. |

(Written by Dr Peter Sloan and Dr Ross Latham for the *First Steps* Project.)

A Problem-Solving Approach to Teaching Explanations

A problem-solving approach to teaching the writing of explanations is an effective way to help Early, Transitional and Conventional writers to improve their written explanations.

Use shared reading sessions to show children different types of explanations, their purposes and who might use them. The following texts can be used as a starting point for children to discuss explanations and to devise a framework that can be refined over time.

The sample texts were written by ten-year-olds and were collected before any discussion about explanation writing. The pupils were asked to write about how the human ear worked. Some had little experience of writing explanations, while others had participated in discussions in health lessons. Their writing reflects their experiences.

Interspersed with the sample texts are the discussion comments of another class of ten-year-olds, together with the teacher's paraphrasing of the children's statements that would later form the basis of a framework and guidelines for the writing of an explanation.

Example 1

Explanation	Pupils said:	Teacher wrote:
The Ear Ears work by collecting sounds and sending them to the brain. They are like funnels. They catch the sounds and bounce them through to the brain where we make sense of them. The tunnels in your ear also go through to your nose, so sometimes if you have a bad cold it can lead to an ear infection.	Example 1 is just one paragraph. The paragraph sort of explains how the ear works, but not precisely. It includes some information that is not needed (the bit about the ear infection).	Not enough information. Too broad. Irrelevant information.

Example 2

Explanation	Pupils said:	Teacher wrote:
How the Ear Works The ear is an organ of the body. There are three parts to the ear — the outer, the middle and the inner. The outer part of the ear is the part that sticks out. It is mostly cartilage and is shaped to collect sound and funnel it into the ear canal. The middle ear is made up of an ear drum and three sound-conducting bones — the hammer, anvil and stirrup. The inner ear is made of a snail-shell shaped tube called the cochlea, which is filled with fluid. Sound goes through the outer ear and vibrates the ear drum which is connected to the hammer. The hammer sends vibrations through the anvil and stirrup into the inner ear. The cochlea changes the vibrations into electric impulses. These go to the brain to be interpreted as sounds. Because the ear has so many sensitive parts, especially the middle and inner ear, it is wise to not stick anything in the ear as damage occurs easily.	I think Example 2 is really effective because it describes the parts, and then clearly tells you how they work together. It uses proper words for each part of the ear. It has a good conclusion.	Describes parts. Clearly explains how parts work. Uses correct vocabulary for the parts. Has an effective conclusion.

Example 3

Explanation	Pupils said:	Teacher wrote:
Ears Your brain makes sense of the noises that come through your ears. There are things in your ear that vibrate when the noises hit them. Before they vibrate they have to be collected in the outside part of your ear, and then they move into the inside part where they make the things vibrate. If you can't hear, then you are deaf. People who are deaf are just born that way.	The title is not very accurate. The author uses *you* and *your* a lot. How the ear works is not clearly explained. The order of how the ear works is muddled. The second paragraph is not really necessary and it is not true.	Title is too broad. No need to include *you* and *your*. Explanation is not clear. The explanation paragraph is not in sequence. Some information irrelevant and inaccurate.

Example 4

Explanation	Pupils said:	Teacher wrote:
Sounds are collected in the outer ear. They vibrate the ear drum and the hammer and the anvil and the stirrup inside the ear, then the cochlea makes the vibrations into electric impulses that are understood by the brain.	The writer doesn't explain what all the parts are — like the hammer, the anvil and the stirrup. The second sentence is too long, so it is hard to follow.	Scientific words not explained. One sentence too long.

The pupils continued to work through the examples making comparisons and comments, which were noted by the teacher. The comments they made indicated that they already had ideas about how explanations should be constructed.

The teacher recorded her comments as follows.

Effective explanations	Ineffective explanations
Title tells how something works. Scientific words are explained and used. How something works is explained in proper sequence. Only relevant information is included. Sentences are clear and easily understood. *You* and *your* are not normally used.	Broad title or no title at all. Vague terms used or scientific words used without prior explanation. The explanation paragraph is poorly sequenced. Irrelevant information included. Sentences are too lengthy or hard to follow. *You* and *your* are used unnecessarily.

The children reviewed their information and constructed their 'Guidelines for Writing Explanations'. It was represented like this:

Guidelines for Writing Explanations

1　Begin with a title that states specifically what the explanation is about.
2　Describe the parts of the thing to be explained.
3　Use and explain specific vocabulary used in the explanation.
4　Explain how things work in a clear sequence.
5　Include relevant information only.
6　Leave out words like 'you' and 'your'.

Planning Frameworks

The planning framework given on page 48 encourages pupils to take notes and begin to write a draft with the framework of an explanation in mind. It is critical that pupils have a solid understanding of the framework and language features before they attempt to use these planning outlines. Pupils need the accumulated learning experiences described in Section 2 of this book to benefit from the planning frameworks.

Pupils need to know that the planning frameworks are intended to make the organisation of a first draft of an explanation easier. Where the frameworks are restrictive, adaptations can be discussed by the pupils and more appropriate outlines developed.

Explanation Plan

TOPIC:
DEFINITION: What is it?
COMPONENTS/PARTS: Describe the components or parts of the object or phenomena being explained.
OPERATIONS: Describe how it works, clarifying cause and effect.
APPLICATIONS: When and where it works or happens or is applied.
EVALUATIVE SUMMARY: (Optional) Are there any special features of the object or phenomena that can be described in a summary of it?

Assessment and Evaluation of Explanation Writing

The Indicators on the following page trace the development of explanation writing. Teachers may choose to use the Indicators to assess pupils' control of explanation writing.

Pupils will rarely display Indicators from only one Phase of Development, so teachers will need to use their professional judgement to determine the main Phase in which the children are working. Directions for the future teaching of explanation writing become evident by examining the next Phase of Development.

Often a pattern of achievement can be detected through the use of the sub-headings, *Purpose, Text Organisation and Content*, and *Language Features*. For example, a group of pupils may exhibit most of the Indicators under the sub-headings *Purpose* and *Text Organisation and Content* in the Consolidating Phase, but also exhibit Indicators under the sub-heading, *Language Features*, in the Beginning Phase. This would suggest that the pupils understand the framework of a set of instructions, but are unaware of the language specific to explanation writing.

EXPLANATION INDICATORS

BEGINNING

Purpose:

The writer:

- discusses cause and effect

Text Organisation and Content

- writes observation and comment, e.g. 'Snow is made from water and it's cold.'

Phenomenon

- makes personal opening statement, e.g. 'I am going to tell how....'
- includes 'is when' in definition, e.g. 'Snow is when...'
- is unable to generalise

Sequence

- explains using subjective language, e.g. 'It makes me feel cold' instead of 'It lowers body temperature.'

Language Features

- uses common connectives, e.g. *and, then*
- includes clichés and slang, e.g. 'It goes as fast as a rocket.'

DEVELOPING

Purpose:

The writer:

- discusses some instances where written explanations are used

Text Organisation and Content

- attempts use of explanation framework

Phenomenon

- attempts generalisations but may revert to specifics

Sequence

- attempts to explain links between cause and effect, e.g. *if... then... because*

Language Features

- begins to use objective language to explain phenomena
- attempts use of passive tense, e.g. *is driven by*
- uses simple present tense, e.g. *happens, turns*
- uses some subject specific terms

CONSOLIDATING

Purpose:

The writer:

- recognises that the purpose of explanations is to explain the way things are or how things work and to give reasons for the phenomenon

Text Organisation and Content

- plans and organises information using a suggested framework

Phenomenon

- is beginning to define terms precisely using 'having', 'being', 'making' verbs
- provides a focus for the reader
- begins to generalise effectively

Sequence

- includes information in logical sequence to explain how or why a phenomenon occurs
- generally explains links between cause and effect
- uses objective language

Language Features

- uses passive voice, e.g. *saturated, is cooled by*
- uses cause and effect linking words , e.g. *if, then, when, why*
- uses simple present tense consistently
- uses a range of subject specific terms

EXTENDING

Purpose:

The writer:

- demonstrates understanding that there are different types of explanations that link cause and effect and to describe processes such as how or why something works
- uses explanations to provide reasons for the appearance of certain phenomena

Text Organisation and Content

- independently plans and organises sufficient information to enable the explanation to be easily followed

Phenomenon

- begins with a clear, precise statement of the phenomenon, e.g. 'Igneous rock is formed when molten rock cools and solidifies'

Sequence

- selects and elaborates appropriate information such as a description of components, how it works or why it works
- effectively links information to clearly demonstrate the relationship of cause and effect
- writes events in logical sequence; includes an evaluation if applicable

Language Features

- uses appropriate subject specific terms and technical vocabulary and includes definition of terms as required
- maintains cohesion through reference to generalised non human participants, e.g. rocks, seasons, land breezes, mountains, combustion, flight
- uses some passives such as *is caused, is affected, are cooled*
- uses linking word to signify cause and effect, e.g. *then, consequently, the result is*

(Adapted from Rivalland, J. and Raison, G. (1990) Education Department of Western Australia: Perth)

Letters, Faxes and E-Mail

Purpose and Types

Letters, faxes and e-mail are forms of written communication rather than text types. Each has many different purposes. Informal letters to a friend or acquaintance may be to recount experiences in a newstelling manner, express feelings or to describe new surroundings. Formal letters may be to an unknown person, or a person in authority, and may be to inquire, complain or request. Faxes and e-mail are just as versatile. They can be used for a range of purposes, too, although the style of the message may be slightly different.

Together with phone calls, letters, faxes and e-mails currently represent the most common way of communicating in both business and social contexts. Yet for all they have in common, there are differences between them that children need to recognise. The table below considers the features of each form of communication, brainstormed by a Year 6 class.

Form	Speed	Privacy	Formality	Cost	Hardware
Phone call	Fast	High	Low	Medium	Phone
Letter	Slow	High	High	Medium	Pen
Fax	Fast	Medium	Medium	Medium	Fax machine
E-mail	Fast	High	Low	Low	Computer

These judgements were based on the pupils' experiences and generalisations. Discussion revolved around matters of distance and time, convenience and cost, which made it difficult to simplify. However, it is important that children have plenty of opportunities to experiment with each form of communication, and discuss the merits of each, as it is a key part of understanding the context of the message.

Letters, faxes and e-mail can be classified in a number of ways. They play an important role in our everyday life and are used in many contexts. One broad way of categorising these texts is as informal and formal. An informal text would generally communicate a matter of a social nature to a known person, such as a friend or acquaintance. A formal text may consist of a simple request that could normally be made orally, but because of the nature of the business to be transacted, and the audience being unknown or a person in authority, is being put in writing.

Informal letters include:

- letters to relatives inquiring about their health and sharing significant events

- faxed reminders to friends

- e-mail sent primarily to maintain social relationships.

Formal letters include:

- complaints sent to companies

- requests for loans

- inquiries about services

- letters to the editor of a newspaper, expressing an opinion.

Another way of classifying letters, faxes and e-mails is to consider them as initiating and responding texts.

An **initiating text** is one sent to someone with the intent of starting an exchange of messages and might:

- pose a question

- request clarification

- recount experiences (inferring readers' interest and hoping for a response).

A **responding text** is essentially a reply and can be:

- an answer to a question

- providing details in response to a request

- a series of comments in response to the writers' experiences ('I'm glad you enjoyed your break…').

In an exchange of messages over a relatively short period of time, most texts have elements of both response and initiation, thereby maintaining the momentum of the written relationship.

Applications Across the Curriculum	An active, community-oriented classroom presents many opportunities for the reading and writing of both formal and informal letters. If community members visit the class and share information about their lives, formal letters of invitation and thanks would be appropriate. If excursions are conducted on a regular basis, arrangements must be made with the proprietors of the venues to be visited.

Not all letter-writing need be for real purposes. Life-like situations often provide a valuable context for the application of letter-writing skills. For example, pupils may be asked to write to a character from a book, persuading them to take a particular course of action.

Here are some examples of how letter-writing can be used across the curriculum:

English	Writing to pen friends
Geography	Writing to groups affected by land use
History	Writing to the elderly about changes in their lifetime

Text Organisation	With the advent of word processing software and alternative means of written communication such as fax and e-mail, the conventions of letter-writing have become less clear. Many variations exist so it can be a worthwhile exercise to ask pupils to collect business letters of a non-private nature for analysis. Pupils can compare and discuss the most common conventions used, and develop guidelines for the writing of letters.

Letter, faxes and e-mails generally have six essential parts.

The address

The address states the location details of the sender, and often the recipient. This may be a postal address, a fax number or an e-mail address, and can be included in a variety of ways. Addresses can form part of a letterhead or a detail list at the top of a fax or e-mail. E-mail addresses can be 'hidden' behind the sender's name, available at the double-click of a mouse. Although the date of a piece of correspondence can be at the opening or closing of a letter, in keeping with faxes and e-mails it appears frequently at the opening, beneath the address.

The greeting or salutation

This can be as formal as *Dear Sir*, or as informal as *Hi Rhonda*. Faxes and e-mails that rely on brevity and directness may rely on the recipient's name being included in the address, and omit the greeting altogether. This appears to be the exception rather than the rule, and generally depends upon a shared understanding between the sender and the recipient.

The need for a prompt, clear response tends to be more apparent in business settings than social ones, particularly in reference to necessary action. Consequently, many fax cover pages include a 'purpose bar' which reads something like:

Please reply ❏ Please forward ❏ For your information ❏ For review ❏ Please recycle ❏

A 'purpose bar' lets the reader know immediately the purpose of the communication, and whether action is required. Often a purpose bar will be accompanied by bars or headings in faxes and e-mails denoting the subject, urgency and/or sensitivity of the matter, again suggesting how the reader should deal with the information. Features such as these allow the recipient to act upon the message swiftly and accurately, and enhance the clarity of the message. They also allow the recipient to sort through large amounts of information efficiently by focusing on key words. For example, a reader scanning e-mail headings will be more interested in the subject heading *FINANCIAL TROUBLE – URGENT* than *GOLF PLANS – WEEKEND.*

The introduction

This states literally or infers the purpose of the communication, and creates a context for the information to follow. For example, a formal letter might begin, 'I am writing to request a copy of the book…'. Stating the purpose so explicitly enables the reader to be clear about the intention of the writer. Although faxes and e-mails are generally briefer and more concise than letters, the opening line is still normally dedicated to stating the purpose and setting the context. Language like 'I'm sorry I haven't contacted you for a while…' and 'I believe congratulations are in order…' infer the reason for the communication, and indicate what sort of information will follow. Where e-mails are being exchanged rapidly between two parties well known to each other, and a single topic is the subject of discussion, replies may render the introduction redundant. However, this situation is relatively rare, and the introduction is seen as essential to letters, faxes and e-mails.

The body

The body of a letter, fax or e-mail may vary dramatically. It may brief enough simply to involve the posing of a question, or lengthy enough to accommodate a life history. Indeed, the technology associated with e-mail means the body of a message can be enhanced by attachments and digital images, among many other things. The body can assume the characteristics of any one of a range of text types, and often a combination of text types or text type components. The paragraph is the most effective unit for organising ideas in this way. There is no limit to the number of paragraphs in the body of a letter, fax or e-mail. Each paragraph generally accommodates one idea (or, in the case of a recount, one event) and links to the surrounding paragraphs. A social letter, for example, often assumes the features of a recount, as the writer recalls the interesting events of the past. Yet a fax from a friend asking how to finish an elaborate piece of craft work might meet with a response that is more of a procedure than a recount, and therefore different in structure. Often, as a way of maintaining social relationships, writers will begin with a collection of personal news items before moving onto more technical matters. In this way two text types could be drawn upon. A letter, fax or e-mail recounting the purchase of an item, which was then described, and its function explained, would involve components of several different text types.

And of course, many letters, faxes and e-mails consist of responses to matters in incoming text. Responding can be structured, assigning each matter raised by the writer a paragraph, or even a number, or informal, embedded in the general text. The software application of e-mails allows a recipient to reply by writing responses between the original text, and simple faxes can be responded to in a similar manner by annotating paragraphs (where space and formality allows it).

The conclusion

Except in the case of single-line messages, most letters, faxes and e-mails have a conclusion. The conclusion normally consists of a restatement of the purpose of the letter and/or a call to action related to the purpose. An effective conclusion begins with a phrase or clause signalling the final part of the message. Common expressions include: *In closing...; In summary; In conclusion...*

The closure

The closure of a letter, fax or e-mail may be a formal farewell such as *Yours sincerely*; a parting gesture of affection such as *Best wishes always*; or a call to action such as *I look forward to your prompt response* (where this has not already been done in the conclusion). In each context the writer's intention is to signal the conclusion of the communication in an appropriate manner. Faxes and e-mails between relative strangers, and dealing with formal matters may omit a closing statement in the interests of brevity, but the name of the sender is generally included.

Prepared formats for letters, faxes and e-mails sometimes make the introduction and closure of communications redundant. Consider the following examples:

- fax sheets that include letterheads and/or footers

- fax sheets that include 'purpose bars' for the sender to tick, e.g. Please respond ❑

- faxes and e-mails that include a subject box for the sender's completion.

Language Features

Letter, faxes and e-mails can possess any of the features of a range of text types because the purpose and context of the communication determine the features of the message. The context includes factors such as:

- the relationship between the writer and reader
- the subject of the message
- the shared understandings between the writer and reader
- the context of the message.

One letter may have many purposes, and therefore incorporate the language features of many different text types. For example, short, sociable e-mails between friends could, due to their informal nature, include the following features:

- pet names
- written in the first person
- inaccurate spelling and handwriting
- use of abbreviations and symbols for shared understandings, e.g. ☺
- clipped language, i.e. *Having a great time* as opposed to *We are having a great time*
- assumed knowledge, e.g. *I'll fix it later…* assuming knowledge of what it refers to.

A formal letter might possess the following features:

- honorific titles, e.g. The Honourable…
- written in the third person
- subject-specific jargon
- structural devices such as paragraphs, tables and diagrams
- legible handwriting
- most words spelled correctly.

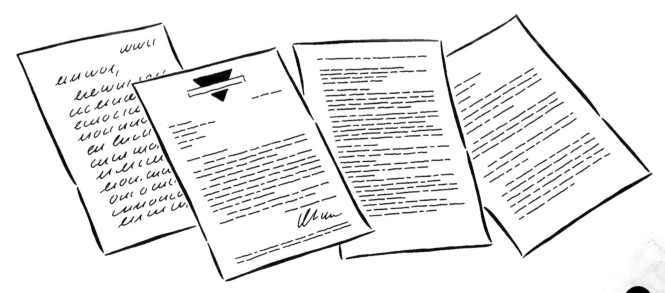

The following charts illustrate the text organisation and language features typical of formal and informal letter-writing.

Formal Letter

Sender's address	20 Hawkswell Gardens Summertown Oxford OX2 7E
Date	2nd September 1999
Receiver's address	The Manager Trendy Televisions P.O. Box 235 Aylesbury Buckinghamshire HP0 2TD
Greeting	Dear Sir/Madam
Purpose of letter	I am writing to complain about the picture quality on the television I bought from your store last week.
Body of letter	The television was delivered and installed by one of your staff and I have not attempted to adjust it, so I believe the problem is with the television. I have phoned your store and asked that someone come and fix it, but was told that the person responsible for the service section is on leave for two weeks. This is just not good enough. I paid a substantial amount of money for that television and expect it to work. If I have not been contacted by the end of this week, I will be contacting the authorities responsible for investigating unfair trading.
Closure	Yours faithfully Ann Oyd

Informal Letter

Sender's address	20 Hawkswell Gardens Summertown Oxford OX2 7E
Date	19th September 1999
Greeting	Dear Ross
Purpose of letter	I just thought I'd drop you a line to let you know how things were working out and see if you were still interested in coming to stay when you visit Britain.
Body of letter	I've settled in well here. The house is near the river, there are shops nearby and the neighbours are good. I've already been to visit a couple of relatives that I have in Aylesbury, and I'm being spoilt rotten. Enough about me, what about you and your family? How is that wicked sister of yours? When I left you were trying to encourage her to get her a job that didn't involve so much travelling. I hope it turned out okay. Pass on my best wishes when you see her next. Things were a bit rushed when I left but you did say you wouldn't mind staying here for a while when you visit Britain in August. There is no hurry about dates and times, it's just that I was planning my own holidays and thought it made sense that the two happen around the same time. When you get a chance, let me know.
Closure	Regards Richard Guest

A Problem-Solving Approach to Teaching Writing Faxes	A problem-solving approach is an effective way to help Early, Transitional and Conventional writers to understand fax writing. Use shared reading sessions to show pupils different types of faxes, their purposes and who might use them.

The following texts can be used as a starting point for children to discuss faxes and to devise a framework that can be refined over time. The example texts are from ten-year-olds and were collected before any discussions about fax writing. The pupils were asked to write to their favourite personality to discover the book most enjoyed by that person as a child. Some had little experience of writing faxes, others had seen examples at home and in other contexts. Their writing reflects their experiences.

Interspersed with the example texts are the discussion comments of another class of ten-year-olds, and how the teacher paraphrased the discussion to write statements that would form the basis of a framework and guidelines for the writing of a fax.

Example 1

Fax	Pupils said:	Teacher wrote:
To: David Beckham Fax number: 0000 000000 Date: 14.6.99	Sample number 1 doesn't include the number of pages.	No page numbers.
Dear Mr Beckham, What is your favourite child's book? From Greg Fax number: 000 000 0000	It needed an introduction. It doesn't give you enough information.	Not enough information.

Example 2

Fax	Pupils said:	Teacher wrote:
To: Tony Blair Fax number: 000 000 0000 From: Marjorie Hummer Date: 15 June 1999 Pages: 1 Subject: Favourite book	Number 2 doesn't have a return fax number. It has the number of pages and the subject of the fax.	Missing a return fax number. Includes the number of pages and the subject of the fax, which makes it easier to read.
Dear Mr Blair, Our class is doing a project where you have to write to someone you really admire and find out what book they liked best when they were little or what child's book they like best now. What's your favourite children's book? From Marjorie Hummer	The first sentence is too long.	Sentences need to be a length that is easy to read.

Example 3

Fax	Pupils said:	Teacher wrote:
To: Michaela Strachan Fax number: 000 000 0000 From: Nimal Wisrasingh Fax number: 000 000 0000 Date: 15 June 1999 Pages: 1 Dear Michaela,	Sample 3 seems to have all the details a fax would need.	Important details for faxes: names, numbers, date and number of pages.
You have been my idol since I saw your first show on TV. What's your favourite children's book? I think you should have your show on more than once a week. Sometimes I have badminton practice and I miss it. My class has to write a fax to a famous person and ask them what their favourite children's book is. What's yours? Yours sincerely Nimal	The information seems to be jumbled up. It has some information that isn't needed. The ending is good.	The information needs to be in paragraphs, and the paragraphs need to be in an order that makes sense. Includes some irrelevant information. The closing (Yours sincerely) is effective.

Example 4

Fax	Pupils said:	Teacher wrote:
To: Cilla Black Fax number: 00000 000000 From: Gael Gibbons Fax number: 000 000 0000 Date: 15 June 1999 Pages: 1 Subject: Your favourite children's book. Dear Cilla,	Sample 4 includes all the stuff a reader needs to know, like names, fax numbers, the date, number of pages and the subject.	Includes all the details a reader needs to know, like names, fax numbers, the date, number of pages and the subject.
My name is Gael Gibbons and I am in Year 5 at Ridge Hill Primary School in Stalybridge. Our class is doing a mini-project where we fax a personality that we like and ask them what their favourite children's book is. It could be one you liked as a child, or one that you've since read, maybe to some children that you know. I am a huge fan of yours and wondered if you could let me know which children's book is your favourite. Thank you for your time. Gael	The author has all the information sorted out so it is easy to read. The first paragraph is good and the ending sounds good.	Information is sorted into paragraphs and put in an order that is easy to follow. Has an effective introduction telling who and where. Has an effective conclusion restating the purpose of the fax.

The pupils continued to work through the samples making comparisons and comments that the teacher jotted down. The comments they made indicated that they already had ideas about how faxes should be constructed.

The teacher recorded her comments like this:

Effective faxes	Ineffective faxes
Include details like names, fax and phone numbers, dates, number of pages and subject.	Leave out essential details like names, fax and phone numbers, dates, number of pages and subject.
Begin with an introduction that outlines the purpose of the fax.	Leave out the introduction.
Have information sorted into paragraphs.	Have information jumbled up.
Have paragraphs in a logical order.	
Have an effective conclusion that restates the purpose of the fax.	Have no conclusion.

The children reviewed their information and constructed their 'Guidelines for Writing Faxes'. It was represented like this:

Guidelines for Writing Faxes

1. Include details like names, fax and phone numbers, dates, number of pages and subject.
2. Begin with an introduction that outlines the purpose of the fax.
3. Sort information into paragraphs.
4. Write paragraphs in a logical order.
5. Write an effective conclusion that restates the purpose of the fax.

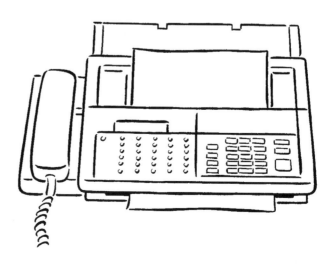

Planning Frameworks

The following planning frameworks encourage pupils to take notes and begin to write a draft with the framework of a letter or fax in mind. It is critical that pupils have a solid understanding of the framework and language features before they attempt to use these planning outlines. Pupils need the accumulated learning experiences described in Section 2 of this book to benefit from the planning frameworks.

Pupils need to know that the planning frameworks are intended to make the organisation of a first draft of a letter or fax easier. Where the frameworks are restrictive, adaptations can be discussed by the pupils and more appropriate outlines developed. The frameworks provide for three paragraphs in the body of the message, although more or less might be appropriate.

Templates for letters, faxes and e-mails are readily available on many pieces of software with word processing capabilities. Where such software and the necessary hardware is available, pupils should be encouraged to use the templates. The following frameworks are suitable for note-taking and the preparation of drafts. A framework has not been provided for e-mails, on the basis that introductory details are entered via software procedures, and the body of an e-mail could consist of a wide range of components.

Formal letter framework

Sender's address and the date	_____ _____ _____ _____
Receiver's address	_____ _____ _____ _____
Greeting	_____
Purpose of letter	_____ _____ _____
Body of letter Paragraph 1	_____ _____ _____ _____
Paragraph 2	_____ _____ _____
Paragraph 3	_____ _____ _____
Conclusion	_____ _____ _____
Closure	_____ _____ _____

Informal letter framework

Sender's address and the date	_____ _____ _____ _____
Greeting	_____
Purpose of letter	_____ _____ _____ _____
Body of letter Paragraph 1	_____ _____ _____ _____
Paragraph 2	_____ _____ _____ _____
Paragraph 3	_____ _____ _____ _____
Conclusion	_____ _____ _____
Closure	_____ _____ _____ _____

Fax framework

Logo and address-	
FACSIMILE TRANSMISSION	
FROM:	TO:
NAME:	NAME:
PHONE:	PHONE:
FAX:	FAX:
DATE:	NUMBER OF PAGES:
SUBJECT:	PRIORITY: ❏ low ❏ medium ❏ urgent

❏ please reply ❏ for your information ❏ action requested ❏ review and return

MESSAGE

_____
_____
_____
_____
_____
_____
_____
_____
_____
_____
_____
_____
_____
_____
_____
_____

Assessment and Evaluation of Transactional Writing

Transactional writing is the term used here to describe written messages between two or more people for a variety of purposes. Letters, postcards, faxes and e-mails are considered to be examples of transactional texts. The Indicators on the following page trace the development of transactional writing. Teachers may choose to use the Indicators to assess pupils' control of transactional writing.

Pupils will rarely display Indicators from only one Developmental Phase, so teachers will need to use professional judgement to determine the main Phase in which the children are working. Directions for the future teaching of transactional writing become evident by examining the next Phase of Development.

Often a pattern of achievement can be detected through the use of the sub-headings, *Purpose, Text Organisation and Content*, and *Language Features*. For example, a group of pupils may exhibit most of the Indicators under the sub-heading *Conventions* in the Consolidating Phase, but also exhibit Indicators under the sub-heading, *Text Organisation and Content*, in the Beginning Phase. This would suggest that the pupils understand the conventions of transactional writing, but are in need of help when shaping the actual message.

TRANSACTIONAL INDICATORS (LETTERS, FAXES, E-MAIL)

BEGINNING

Purpose
The writer:
- writes simple messages for immediate audiences

Purpose

Text Organisation and Content
- writes a purposeful message with limited description
- sometimes sequences events
- writes simple messages for family and friends
- writes messages linked to action (requests), events (recounts) and social relationships (description of feelings)

Conventions
- may copy or adapt significant layout or conventions associated with letters, postcards, greeting cards, faxes or e-mails

Mode
experiments with various modes of delivery

Language Features
- uses oral language structures
- often assumes prior knowledge of reader
- includes first person references

Language Features
- begins to use formal language structures e.g. In the playgroundÖ todayÖ
- provides adequate background detail

DEVELOPING

Purpose
The writer:
- writes detailed messages for a growing range of audiences

Purpose

Text Organisation and Content
- writes a detailed message that may include irrelevant detail
- sequences events using simple references to time, e.g. Before lunchÖ After we got home
- writes detailed messages that sometimes lack cohesion for audiences outside immediate family and friends
- writes about familiar and unfamiliar subjects

Conventions
- recognises and uses basic conventions associated with letters, faxes and e-mails

Mode
- begins to recognise the features and advantages of various modes of delivery

Text Organisation and Content
- writes clear and ordered messages for a range of audiences
- uses paragraph structure and references to time to sequence events
- writes detailed, cohesive messages for a variety of audiences
- can respond to messages and maintain the momentum of a written relationship e.g. pen pal exchange

Language Features
- uses the formal and informal language appropriately
- caters for an unfamiliar audience by providing background information where necessary

CONSOLIDATING

Purpose
The writer:
- uses letters, faxes and e-mails for general written communication

Purpose

Conventions
- recognises and uses a range of accepted conventions associated with letters, faxes and e-mails

Mode
- chooses the most appropriate mode of delivery based on purpose, audience and form

Text Organisation and Content
- writes clear, ordered and concise messages for a wide range of audiences
- uses paragraph structure and subtle references to time to sequence events
- writes messages that incorporate an introduction, body and conclusion
- uses letters, faxes and e-mails to initiate and maintain business and social relationships, and solve problems

Language Features
- conveys appropriate tone through the choice of words and style adopted
- anticipates the readerís needs and supplies supporting detail

EXTENDING

Purpose
The writer:
- uses letters, faxes and e-mails discriminately to maintain business / social relationships and solve problems

Conventions
- manipulates and selects conventions of letters, faxes and e-mails to enhance the message

Mode
- selects and combines modes of delivery to maximise the exchange of messages, e.g. faxes a document due to urgency; follows up with a posted version due to legality

<table>
<tr><td>

Recounts

Purpose and Types

</td><td>

The purpose of a recount is to retell or recount past experiences. Recounts that are based on the direct experiences of the author are sometimes called personal narratives. Non-fiction recounts generally retell accounts of lives, journeys, processes and events with an emphasis on objectivity. Imaginative recounts relate fictitious events, e.g. 'A day in the life of a coin'.

</td></tr>
</table>

Applications Across the Curriculum

Because any notable event can be retold (verbally) or recounted in written form, there are many opportunities for recount writing across the curriculum. To ensure that the writing is meaningful, a clear and motivating purpose and audience is vital. Writing a recount for someone who has shared the experience first-hand, for example, lacks authenticity. Writing a recount as part of a letter to a pen friend, or as a result of recording the memoirs of war veterans, however, is meaningful.

A recount is arguably the most appropriate text type for reflective writing. Teachers who have taught pupils to use a learning journal to reflect on their understandings have declared the simple, but ordered structure of a recount a successful means of helping pupils sort out their thoughts.

Here are some examples of how recount writing can be used across the curriculum:

English	Biographies, autobiographies
Social Studies	Diaries of explorers
Maths	Journal entry: How I found the area of the irregular shape*
Health	Diary of food and exercise
Science	Recount of a field trip

* Note that this recount may read like an instructional text in the past tense, and the differences between the two text types should be made clear to pupils.

Text Organisation

- The introductory information of a recount normally includes details of who, what, where, when, how and why. This information is the setting or orientation and it serves the purpose of orienting the reader. For example:

> On Tuesday, 16th February, 1999, the Year 5 class at Ridgehill School began their journey to Torquay.

Elements of the setting are included or omitted depending on their importance. The following introduction has who, when, where, what and why:

> On March 10, 1876, Alexander Graham Bell, a 29-year-old Scotsman, and his assistant, Thomas Watson, worked busily in a tiny laboratory in Boston, Massachusetts, preparing batteries, cables and wires for an experiment. Bell and his assistant were trying to create what they called a harmonic telegraph, and ended up inventing the telephone.

- The body of a recount consists of key events, which are arranged in chronological order. Each key event is described in detail, and often forms a paragraph. The paragraphs are joined by signal phrases and linking sentences. For example:

  - repetition/reference: e.g. *Young Charles was more interested in the natural world and spent much of his time studying the differences and changes in living things.* **The interest in nature** *continued into his time …*

  - chronology: e.g. *…the survivors were washed up on the shores of a remote island.* **At first light***…*

  - linking, comparing or contrasting ideas: e.g. *…as a result of her discoveries she found fame and moderate wealth.* **However**, *good health continued to elude her, and in 1862…*

- Most recounts have an evaluative comment or concluding statement.

Language Features	Recounts generally:

Recounts generally:

- include specific participants

- are written in simple past tense

- include many verbs

- use linking words or phrases to link sentences and paragraphs.

(Adapted from Derewianka, B. (1990) *Exploring How Texts Work*)

> In the Easter Holidays
>
> I went to Olivias House to Sleep night.
>
> Olivia asked me to because my brother was asked to sleep by Olivias brothers
>
> I felt very happy because at home I have never got any body to Play with at home. It was very Exiting because we walked Olivia's dog Nevile He's a Kern terrier
>
> I walked Nevle in the field. Nevile chased all the dogs and went down the stream We had to call him out.
>
> My brother killed a rat.
>
> THE END

A Year 4 recount about a holiday visit

The following chart illustrates the organisation and language features typical of a recount.

Setting	Charles Darwin was a 19th century scientist whose ideas had a huge impact on the way people think about the world. Although he was born in England, Darwin travelled the world studying animal behaviour.
Event 1	Charles Darwin was born in Shrewsbury, England, in 1809. As a child he disliked school and did poorly. This was a great disappointment to his father, who was a doctor. Young Charles was more interested in the natural world and spent much of his time studying the differences and changes in living things.
Event 2	The interest in nature continued into his time at Cambridge University, where he was studying religion, and triggered a decision, at the age of 22, to join the crew of HMS *Beagle* as Ship's Naturalist. HMS *Beagle* was to sail around the world, and Darwin's job was to collect specimens of plants, animals and rocks.
Event 3	On his travels, Darwin was particularly fascinated by animals which had developed amazing behaviours to survive in a new environment. On his return to England he used his collection of specimens as the basis for a book called *The Origin of the Species*. In this book he concluded that over many years, as the environment changed, some animals adapted and others did not. His name for this process was 'natural selection'.
Conclusion	Darwin's ideas upset some people who suggested that he was denying the existence of God and the explanations of the Bible. His thinking had challenged the beliefs commonly held about life. Darwin's Theory of Evolution as it came to be known, is still discussed rigorously today by scientists and common people unlike.

A Problem-Solving Approach to Teaching Recounts

A problem-solving approach to teaching the writing of recounts is an effective way to help Early, Transitional and Conventional writers to improve their written recounts. Use shared reading sessions to show children different types of recounts, their purposes and who might use them.

The following texts can be used as a starting point for children to discuss recounts and to devise a framework that can be refined over time. The example texts are from nine-year-olds and were collected after a trip to an ice cream factory. Interspersed with the texts are the discussion comments of another class of nine-year-olds, and how the teacher paraphrased the discussion to write statements that would form the basis of a framework and guidelines for the writing of a recount.

Example 1

Recount	Pupils said:	Teacher wrote:
A Good Day We went to an ice cream factory and I got a free hat and an ice cream. The video was good. The factory was good. The bus ride was boring. The day was good. I wanted to go in the freezer but I couldn't go in because I wasn't allowed. I picked a drumstick and the cone was crunchy.	Sample 1 is the worst because the title wasn't any help and it didn't say who went to the factory or when they went. It didn't really tell you what happened. Things were out of order. It shouldn't have the bit about wanting to go in the freezer.	Title doesn't tell enough. Not enough information given about the setting. Events were not mentioned in order. Some irrelevant details were included.

Example 2

Recount	Pupils said:	Teacher wrote:
A Visit We went to an ice cream factory. We caught the bus and the driver was making jokes. Some kids were a bit noisy so the teacher told them off. The bus ride was good. It started to rain just when we got near the place but it stopped when we were getting out. The first thing was getting a free hat then watching a video. After that we walked around the factory and some kids were allowed to taste some new ice cream. Patricia, Felicity and Jan tasted it. The machines were big and some ladies were putting stuff in boxes and they had hats on so their hair couldn't get in anything. I got a free ice cream and then we went home.	I think number 2 is okay, but the first bit is all about the bus ride. It doesn't tell how the ice cream is made. It doesn't give much detail.	Gets off the subject. Leaves out important information. Lacks description.

Example 4

Recount	Pupils said:	Teacher wrote:
Our Visit to an Ice Cream Factory Yesterday the children from Room 10 went by bus to the ice cream factory to find out how ice cream was made. When we arrived we all got a free hat and then watched a video about making ice cream. The lady showed us some new products and some people were allowed to taste them. I didn't like the Green Tea ice cream at all! After the video session we split into two groups and a lady showed us around the factory and explained how ice cream was made. It was quite interesting to look through the windows but we couldn't get near the ice creams. I found out that they export a lot of ice cream to other countries. Before we left we went to the cafeteria and were allowed to choose a free ice cream. We all sat on the lawn and ate it. My ice cream was a chocolate drumstick. It was delicious. As soon as everyone had finished eating, we got on the bus and went back to school. It was a long day, but we learnt a lot about ice creams.	Example number 3 is the best because the title helps us to know what the recount is about and important information about who, when, where, what and why are in the first sentence. It tells all the things they did. Each bit tells us about a different part of the trip. Each paragraph begins with words that tell when things happened. Each part of the recount includes bits about how the writer felt, like what was interesting, what was delicious etc. The recount has a conclusion that summarises the day.	Title summarises the text. Setting includes information that tells who, when, where, what and why. Events are described in time order. Each paragraph is on a different part of the topic. Each paragraph begins with a phrase that indicates time. The writer included descriptions of events and the emotions these events triggered. The conclusion includes a summary of the recount.

The pupils continued to work through the samples making comparisons and comments that the teacher jotted down. The comments they made indicated that they already had ideas about how recounts should be constructed.

The teacher recorded her comments like this:

Effective recounts	Ineffective recounts
Have an accurate title. Include who, when, where, what and why in the setting. Are in proper sequence. Include only the important information. Use a variety of sentence beginnings. Have all the necessary information. Have paragraphs that indicate changes in time. Describe events clearly. Include a conclusion that summarises and/or evaluates the events.	Have an unrelated title or no title at all. Have a setting without all the necessary elements. Have events out of proper sequence. Have irrelevant information. Overuse *and* and *then* as sentence beginnings. Leave out important information. Leave out time references. Lack description of events. Leave out the conclusion or essential parts of it.

The children reviewed their information and constructed their 'Guidelines for Writing Recounts'. It was represented like this:

Guidelines for Writing Recounts

1 Begin with a title that describes what the recount is about.
2 Include who, when, where, what and why in the setting.
3 Describe events in time order.
4 Include only the important information.
5 Use a variety of sentence beginnings.
6 Have all the necessary information.
7 Have paragraphs that indicate changes in time.
8 Describe events clearly.
9 Include a conclusion that summarises and/or evaluates the events.

Planning Framework

The planning framework below encourages pupils to take notes and begin to write a draft with the framework of a recount text in mind. It is critical that pupils have a solid understanding of the text organisation and language features before they attempt to use planning frameworks. Pupils need the accumulated learning experiences described in Section 2 of this book before they can fully benefit from the use of planning frameworks.

Pupils need to know that planning frameworks are intended to make the organisation of a first draft of a recount text easier. Where the frameworks are restrictive, adaptations can be discussed by the pupils and more appropriate outlines developed.

Recount Plan

Setting Who? When? Where? What? Why?	_____
Event 1	_____
Event 2	_____
Event 3	_____
Conclusion	_____

Assessment and Evaluation of Recount Writing

The Indicators on the following page trace the development of recount writing. Teachers may choose to use the Indicators to assess pupils' control of recount writing.

Pupils will rarely display Indicators from only one Developmental Phase, so teachers will need to use professional judgement to determine the main Phase in which the children are working. Directions for the future teaching of recount writing become evident by examining the next Phase of Development.

Often a pattern of achievement can be detected through the use of the sub-headings, *Purpose, Text Organisation and Content*, and *Language Features*. For example, a group of pupils may exhibit most of the Indicators under the sub-headings *Purpose* and *Text Organisation and Content* in the Consolidating Phase, but also exhibit Indicators under the sub-heading, *Language Features*, in the Beginning Phase. This would suggest that the pupils understand the framework of a set of instructions, but are unaware of the language specific to recount writing.

RECOUNT INDICATORS

Recounts

BEGINNING

Purpose:

The writer:
- uses recounts to tell of a past experience

Text Organisation and Content
- writes a simple account with little description

Orientation
- provides little information about setting or the context in which the events happened, e.g. tells who and where but not when.

Events
- uses oral language structures, gives all events equal attention and importance, e.g. Dawn-to-dark accounts—'I got up. I went to the zoo. I came home.'
- links events chronologically

Evaluation (optional)
- writes an evaluative comment as a conclusion

Language Features
- uses oral language structures
- usually writes in the past tense
- uses little variety of linking words, e.g. *and, then*

DEVELOPING

Purpose:

The writer:
- uses recounts to reconstruct past events

Text Organisation and Content
- establishes time, place and participants of recount and includes events in sequence

Events
- writes additional information about more important events, e.g. 'My dad took me to the zoo. I saw all the animals. The elephant was the biggest and best animal. I liked the monkeys too. When it was dark, we went home.'
- includes only characters of significance to the recount

Evaluation (optional)
- writes a satisfactory conclusion

Language Features
- begins to use structures of written language
- uses some adverbs and adjectives to clarify meaning
- maintains tense
- uses action verbs and generally shows agreement between subject and verb, e.g. *I went, I saw, I did*
- uses a limited number of linking words, e.g. *and so, later, soon*
- writes complete sentences
- uses a variety of sentence lengths

CONSOLIDATING

Purpose:

The writer:
- demonstrates understanding that recounts can retell a personal experience, record particulars of an event, e.g. a football match, be an imaginative description of events
- demonstrates understanding that diaries, news reports, biographies, journals, may be recounts

Text Organisation and Content
- provides an orientation that is complete and succinct and includes significant events in chronological sequence

Orientation
- caters for reader by providing contextual details
- provides details of the environment that impact on the way events unfold

Events
- attempts to interpret events imaginatively, elaborating important events
- elaborates aspects of characters that affect events
- gives characters credibility by use of dialogue or significant actions, e.g. Mum said angrily, 'Come here at once!'
- sustains topic throughout

Evaluation (optional)
- writes more complex concluding statements with evaluative comment or summary

Language Features
- uses a variety of appropriate adjectival and adverbial phrases
- maintains consistent past tense
- uses a variety of action and process verbs, e.g. *I travelled, I glimpsed, I thought*
- varies conjunctions and linking words to indicate time, e.g. *soon, later, eventually*
- writes complete sentences that are increasingly complex
- groups sentences containing related information into paragraphs

EXTENDING

Purpose:

The writer:
- demonstrates understanding that recounts can be written for a number of purposes and audiences and that a writer's experiences influence what he/she writes

Text Organisation and Content
- organises the schematic structure of the recount by starting with an orientation that aims to interest the reader and including important events relating to a particular occasion

Orientation
- includes all relevant background information needed to understand the text, i.e. who was involved, when and where it happened and other pertinent details

Events
- develops the topic fully by including significant events chosen to add interest and impact
- elaborates events so that the reader is able to visualise the experience
- interprets events imaginatively, symbolically or metaphorically
- orders the events chronologically into easily followed sequential steps
- sometimes includes personal reflections or comments about events in the recount, e.g. it was a great honour....

Evaluation (optional)
- writes a concluding comment that contains evaluative comment and summarises aspects of the recount

Language Features
- writes about specific participants
- writes cohesively using a variety of linking words to do with time, e.g. *next, after, subsequently, the following day, meanwhile*
- uses a variety of sentence beginnings to make the recount more interesting
- maintains simple past tense or manipulates tense

(Adapted from Rivalland, J. and Raison, G. (1990) Education Department of Western Australia: Perth)

Reports	The purpose of a report is to systematically organise and record factual information to classify and describe a whole class of things.

| ***Purpose and Types*** | There are many contexts in which people are asked to write reports. Many of these, like newspaper reports, bear a greater resemblance in structure and style to a recount. In the context of this book, reports refer to factual texts that classify and describe a class of things.

The structure of a report is dictated by its purpose, context and content. For example, a report about reptiles might include a classification paragraph, and information about appearance, habitat and behaviour. A report about pioneer women, however, would have information about social status, housing and health. |
|---|---|

Applications Across the Curriculum	All areas of the curriculum involve the reading and writing of reports. Any class of things can be described in the body of a report. Therefore the following subject matter could be used in the reading and writing of reports.

Social Studies	A particular cultural group
Health	A major organ
Science	An animal or plant
Physical Education	A particular sport
Art	A class (style) of painters

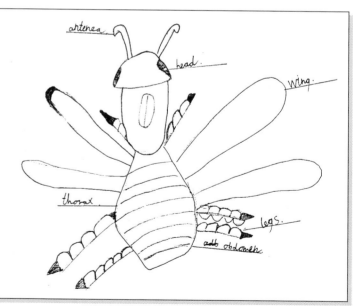

The honey bee

The bee is an insect because it has six legs. It is an invertebrate because its hasn't got a back b. The honey bee got 3 parts to the body and it is the thorax and the haed and the abdomen.

A bee will sting you because it is protects their body. Then they will die. An honey bee has bright yellow and orange body. An honey bee lives in different clustrys and they live everywhere.

Bees lives in holes and trees. If you nall them all crawl them they will sting you. Some honey bees are camouflage to the grass, because they are black and orange.

artenea. head. wing. thorat legs. add obdomeh.

Aaron (Year 3) wrote a report on the honey bee.

Text Organisation	A report generally has three main components. Each stage has a separate and distinct function.

- The **generalisation** or **classification** states what the subject is (e.g. snakes are reptiles) or orients the reader with some reference which leads to a generalisation (e.g. few ball sports have the same popularity worldwide as football).

- The **description** makes up the body of the report. Aspects described will vary according to the content and context of the report. For example, when writing a report about an animal, it is common practice to allocate a paragraph to appearance (what it looks like), location (where it lives and, if necessary, a reference to time) and dynamics (what it does). These paragraphs collectively constitute the description. On the other hand, a report about a type of computer might include paragraphs about components and dynamics, but have no need for any information related to location.

- The final and optional element of a report is the **summarising comment**. The summarising comment is sometimes omitted because an element of the description serves the purpose of a conclusion. For example, a report about polar bears might conclude with a paragraph about location that discusses the effects of global warming on the habitat and therefore the future of polar bears.

Language Features	Report texts are characterised by the following language features:

- generalised non-human participants (the motor, volcanoes, currents)

- descriptive language, but factual and precise rather than imaginative

- mainly action verbs (falls, rises, changes)

- timeless present tense (are, happens, turns)

- language for defining, classifying, comparing and contrasting (are called, belong to, can be classified as, are similar to, are more powerful than)

- likely to contain technical vocabulary

- the writing is in a relatively formal objective style – the use of first person pronouns (I, we) and the writer's opinions are not generally appropriate to this type of writing.

(Adapted from Derewianka, B. (1990) *Exploring How Texts Work*)

The following chart illustrates the text organisation and language features characteristic of reports.

Text organisation	The Honey Bee	Language features
Classification/ Generalisation What is the subject of the report?	The honey bee is an insect.	Generalised participants: a whole class of things – *The honey bee…* Could also read *Honey bees…*
Description: appearance What does it look like?	The honey bee is bright yellow and orange. It is 12mm long and has six legs. The honey bee has three separate parts to its body.	Many 'linking' verbs (is, has) in timeless present tense Descriptive language that is factual and precise rather than imaginative
Description: location Where does it live?	This insect lives in most parts of the world.	A relatively formal, objective style – absence of *I, we*, and opinions
Description: dynamics What does it do?	These bees collect nectar for honey. They dance on the honeycomb to show the other bees where the best flowers for honey are. Honey bees may fly 200,000km to collect enough nectar for 500g of honey.	Some subject-specific vocabulary appropriate to purpose and audience – *nectar, honeycomb*
Summarising comment	Bees are social insects that play a very important role in the pollination of flowers.	Timeless present tense

(Adapted from material written by Dr Peter Sloan and Dr Ross Latham for the *First Steps* Project.)

<table>
<tr><td>

A Problem-Solving Approach to Teaching Report Writing

</td><td>

A problem-solving approach to teaching the writing of reports is an effective way to help Early, Transitional and Conventional writers to improve their reports.

</td></tr>
</table>

Use shared reading sessions to show children different types of reports, their purposes and who might use them. The example texts below can be used as a starting point for children to discuss instructions and to devise a framework that can be refined over time. The texts were written by ten-year-olds and were collected before any discussions about report writing. The pupils were asked to write what they knew about frogs. Some knew little about frogs, while others had encountered information both at home and at school. Their writing reflects their experiences.

Interspersed with the example texts are the discussion comments of another class of ten-year-olds, and the teacher's paraphrasing of their statements that would later form the basis of a framework and guidelines for the writing of a report.

Example 1

Report	Pupils said:	Teacher wrote:
Frogs I reckon frogs are good. They have big bulging eyes and they jump. Frogs are covered with wet skin or they die. Frogs live in trees or in water or in burrows. Frogs croak. The male ones croak really loud but the females don't. They can be big or little.	Lots of information but a bit hard to follow.	Information needs to be organised and easy to follow.

Example 2

Report	Pupils said:	Teacher wrote:
Frogs Frogs are slippery and slimy. They can jump a long way. They croak. They have wet skin. They hide sometimes. Their eyes are very big and I know some people who are scared of them. I am not scared of them. I think they are very cute. That's what I think!	Includes too many opinions. Includes feelings towards frogs instead of describing them.	Reports should be factual. Irrelevant information included.

Example 3

Report	Pupils said:	Teacher wrote:
Frogs The frog is a small amphibious animal. Amphibians spend part of their life on land and part in water. Frogs have large back legs, short front legs and a flattish body with no neck. Most frogs have a sticky tongue that is attached to the front of the mouth. When they want food (like insects), they can flip the tongue out. Frogs have wet skin with no hair. Some frogs change colour and can be camouflaged from their enemies. Frogs lay eggs, in jelly, and these hatch into tadpoles. Tadpoles change gradually into frogs. This is called metamorphosis. Frogs are useful to humans because frogs eat insects.	Each paragraph is about something different to do with frogs. Has lots of extra information. Uses special words like 'amphibious' and 'camouflaged'. Varies sentence beginnings — not always Frogs... Frogs...	Information is organised into paragraphs. Includes plenty of detail. Uses some subject-specific vocabulary. Varies sentence beginnings — not always Frogs... Frogs...

Example 4

Report	Pupils said:	Teacher wrote:
Frogs Frogs are animals. They live in water. They eat insects. They can be small (1 centimetre) or big (30 centimetres). Frogs and toads are different. Frogs are in a lot of magic stories. Frogs can jump a long way. Frogs can lay eggs and these eggs can float in the water and then they can turn into tadpoles and they get legs and then they are frogs. Frogs have to keep their skin wet or they die. Some people eat frog's legs but I wouldn't. What I like about frogs is their eyes. They are big and round and sticky-out. Frogs and toads are a bit the same and a bit different. Frogs are good because they eat insects. Toads have warts.	Has lots of information but it is not well organised. Mixes some facts with some opinions. Repeats some words — then they, then they...	Information isn't easy to find. Reports need to be factual. Needs to include linking words and phrases.

The pupils continued to work through the samples making comparisons and comments, which were noted by the teacher. The comments they made indicated that they already had ideas about how reports should be constructed.

The teacher recorded her comments like this:

Effective reports	**Ineffective reports**
Information is organised into paragraphs and easy to follow. Include only relevant, factual material. Use subject-specific vocabulary. Vary sentence beginnings and connecting words or phrases.	Information written randomly: no grouping of ideas. Mix opinions with facts and irrelevant details. Use colloquial words to describe subject (sticky-out). Repeat sentence beginnings and connecting phrases.

The children reviewed their information and constructed their 'Guidelines for Writing Reports'.

It was represented like this:

Guidelines for Writing Reports

1   Organise information into paragraphs.
2   Include facts not opinions.
3   Vary sentence beginnings and connecting phrases.
4   Use subject-specific vocabulary.
5   Leave out words like 'I', 'we' and 'think'.

Planning Frameworks

The following planning framework can be used to encourage pupils to take notes and begin to write a draft with the framework of a report in mind. It is critical that pupils have a solid understanding of the framework and language features before they attempt to use these planning outlines. Pupils need the accumulated learning experiences described in Section 2 of this book before they can benefit from the planning frameworks.

Pupils need to know that planning frameworks are intended to make the organisation of a first draft of a report easier. Where the frameworks are restrictive, adaptations can be discussed by the pupils and more appropriate outlines developed.

Recount Plan

Title:	
Headings	Short notes
Classification What is it?	
Description: appearance	
Description: place and time	
Description: dynamics	
Summarising comment	

(Adapted from material written by Dr Peter Sloan and Dr Ross Latham for the *First Steps* Project.)

Assessment and Evaluation of Report Writing

The Indicators on the following page trace the development of report writing. Teachers may choose to use the Indicators to assess pupils' control of report writing.

Pupils will rarely display Indicators from only one Developmental Phase, so teachers will need to use professional judgement to determine the main Phase in which the children are working. Directions for the future teaching of report writing become evident by examining the next Phase of Development.

Often a pattern of achievement can be detected through the use of the sub-headings, *Purpose, Text Organisation and Content*, and *Language Features*. For example, a group of pupils may exhibit most of the Indicators under the sub-headings *Purpose* and *Text Organisation and Content* in the Consolidating Phase, but also exhibit Indicators under the sub-heading, *Language Features*, in the Beginning Phase. This would suggest that the pupils understand the framework of a report, but are unaware of the language specific to report writing.

Reports

REPORT INDICATORS

BEGINNING	DEVELOPING	CONSOLIDATING	EXTENDING
Purpose:	**Purpose:**	**Purpose:**	**Purpose:**
The writer:	The writer:	The writer:	The writer:
• discusses the purpose of written reports	• discusses the purpose of written reports	• demonstrates understanding that reports are written to provide information	• demonstrates understanding that there are different types of reports and that the structure of a report depends on the purpose for which it is written • demonstrates understanding that reports contain information that is selected, sorted and synthesised to give the reader/writer information significant to a topic or focus of study
Text Organisation and Content	**Text Organisation and Content**	**Text Organisation and Content**	**Text Organisation and Content**
• writes observation and comment or a recount	• uses part of the report framework	• uses report framework	• uses report framework and adapts it to suit purpose and audience
Classification	*Classification*	*Classification*	*Classification*
• sometimes attempts to generalise and classify information	• introduces the topic • writes a classification that lacks precision • attempts to generalise • uses some generic terms, e.g. *people, animals*	• writes an introduction with a generalisation and/or classification	• writes an introduction that successfully classifies and/or generalises information essential to the subject of the report • uses accurate definitions
Description	*Classification*	*Description*	*Descriptions*
• focuses on a specific part of a whole class of things, e.g. 'My cat eats meat' not 'Cats eat meat.' • includes features that are not necessarily important or relevant	• attempts a classification or generalisation *Description* • gives limited general information in description • is beginning to organise aspects of topics into paragraphs • selects some important aspects to elaborate • describes some specific features • attempts to classify information gathered	• includes some accurate, detailed description of the subject, e.g. size, colour, other features • is able to select and elaborate special features • includes detail that is clearly related to the topic • attempts to make comparisons that help the reader visualise aspects of the subject, e.g. 'It looked like an enormous lizard.' • classifies information effectively for use	• includes detailed information selected because of its relevance to the subject of the report • elaborates on and interprets important information • organises like information into paragraphs that link cohesively in logical order
Conclusion		*Conclusion*	*Conclusion*
• writes a concluding statement that is a comment rather than a summary of the report	*Conclusion* • uses a simple concluding statement with some attempt to summarise what has been written	• writes a summary or concluding paragraph that includes main features of the report, e.g. 'This invention will change the course of history.'	• writes a conclusion that accurately identifies the main points
Language Features	**Language Features**	**Language Features**	**Language Features**
• uses personal or subjective language, e.g. 'I really like...' • writes a simple description with few refined adjectives, e.g. *big, little* • uses simple conjunctions such as *and* • has difficulty maintaining simple present tense • shows little evidence of writing in the third person • writes statements about the 'here and now', e.g. 'My cat like to chase birds.'	• is beginning to use written language structures e.g. 'Pollution has invaded....' • uses some technical or subject specific vocabulary • uses simple conjunctions, such as *and, so, because* • is beginning to use linking verbs, such as *is, a, has a, belongs to* • is beginning to use timeless verbs, e.g. *fight, climb* • is beginning to use timeless present tense • is beginning to maintain third person	• organises aspects of topics into paragraphs • uses precise subject specific vocabulary • uses linking verbs effectively • uses timeless action verbs effectively, e.g. *suckle, teach, fight, climb* • maintains timeless present tense throughout • maintains third person stance throughout	• writes using a formal and objective style • demonstrates consistent use of tense (usually timeless present tense), e.g. *are, hunt, fly, live, suckle* • demonstrates consistent use of singular or plural generic participants, e.g. *humanity faces increasing..., the family is....* • uses generic terms successfully, e.g. *humankind, mammals, pollutants* • uses a range of precise subject-specific terms in context • uses precise descriptive language • uses linking verbs, e.g. *has a, is a, belongs to* • uses appropriate language to compare, contrast, define or classify, e.g. *identical, related, kindred*

(Adapted from Rivalland, J. and Raison, G. (1990) Education Department of Western Australia: Perth)

Broad Contexts for Teaching Text Types

The teaching of text types can be viewed from a broad or specific perspective. Clearly pupils who have had limited experience reading or writing a text form may require teaching over a period of at least four weeks to become aware of the purpose, structure and language features of that text type. The contexts discussed here belong to that broad, long-term perspective, and are global and versatile enough to be used just as easily to teach a writing or a reading skill. The strategies described as *before, during* and *after* strategies, however, are considered more specific – not because their outcomes are short-lived, but because they are used before, during and after the acts of reading or writing. That is, these strategies are more specific in their purpose, and are designed to be the focus of a lesson or series of lessons. Teachers can benefit from both perspectives, keeping in mind that many specific strategies can be used within a broad context (e.g. brainstorming as part of a shared writing session), or as a sequel to them (e.g. text innovation after a guided reading session). The Literacy Hour provides an ideal framework for this cohesive approach to teaching children about text types.

Teachers can use a broad sequence of strategies to explore the structure and language features of information texts. The Literacy Hour offers an ideal context in which to undertake the essential shared and guided reading and modelled and shared writing that underpin the teaching of a text type. Detailed explanations of modelled, shared and guided reading and writing are given in the *First Steps* book *Shared and Guided Reading and Writing at Key Stage 2.* The Literacy Hour also offers many opportunities to explore language features and grammatical structures when teachers are focusing on the necessary word and sentence features of a text. Activities and strategies designed for use in the Literacy Hour can be found in the book *Word and Sentence Work at Key Stage 2.*

Children also encounter and explore text forms beyond the Literacy Hour, in a variety of contexts such as science – explanations and procedures; geography – reports and explanations; history – reports and recounts.

When pupils are familiar with a specific text form, with guidance, they can talk about and identify the elements of the text through discussion and problem-solving. Elements are listed and used as a basis for comparing a range of similar text forms. The list may need to be amended as children interact with text, as they should not be expected to get everything right first time round.

It is important that children are given opportunities to identify structures and features of a text form through problem-solving. In the long term, it is not helpful to give them a format which they are expected to follow. If they are challenged to work things out for themselves, they will never forget their findings, whereas if they are provided with the ready-made 'crutch' of a blueprint to follow, many will not remember or use it spontaneously in their reading or writing.

Knowledge of a text type and of the language features it embodies is essential both for the reading and writing of a form. Although this knowledge is acquired gradually over time and becomes more sophisticated as pupils mature, no assumptions about previous knowledge should be made. In Key Stage 2 some children begin to refine their understandings. The Text Types Continua provide invaluable guides for teachers who need to trace pupils' development of control over the forms and who might find the listed structure and language features useful when planning a teaching programme.

Reading comprehension is greatly enhanced if children are able to use the structure of the text to help them know what to expect. For instance, by realising that the introductory sentence or paragraph of a report contains the essence of what is to follow, they are able to predict content and organise their thinking. An understanding of language features, and of why a text type uses specific features, also greatly enhances comprehension.

Writing a text form demands a clear understanding of structure, format and linguistic features. Understanding deepens and extends as children mature, but even Year 3 children are capable of knowing the features of a recount or a simple report.

The following steps are used to introduce children to the structures and features of non-fiction text forms:

1 Familiarisation

2 Identifying language features and structure of the text

3 Modelling the text form

4 Reading comprehension activities

5 Shared and guided reading

6 Shared and guided writing

7 Teaching vocabulary and sentence structure

8 Independent reading and writing

9 Sharing and reflecting.

Familiarisation

Teachers first set up the context and purpose for teaching a text form. Teachers familiarise children with many simple examples of the text form across a variety of classroom contexts. For example:

- through shared reading in the Literacy Hour, using an information text published as a big book

- by modelling the writing of a text either in the Literacy Hour, or during appropriate lessons in a range of different subject areas, e.g. reports in science, procedures in art

- by borrowing examples of the text form from other classes, or by bringing other examples such as those contained in a magazine or local newspaper.

Familiarisation should start long before the formal teaching of a text type is undertaken. If a Year 3 teacher reads simple reports and recounts to children, this gives them a head start when they move into the following years. It is essential that a good balance is maintained between fiction and non-fiction. Because children are familiar with a text type, they are able to think and talk about structures and features as easily as they can discuss the characters and plots of stories.

Identifying Language Features and Structure of the Text	When teaching a specific text form, teachers talk with children about the purpose, intended audiences and topics of many examples of the same text form. After shared and guided reading and writing, the teacher and children talk about and list the component parts and language features of a text. Using the children's words, guidelines are gradually developed for reading and writing a recount, procedure, explanation or report effectively. The teacher writes the guidelines suggested by the children onto strips of card or a large chart. Examples from the text are noted, e.g. *Reports have facts – Spiders have eight legs.*

The guidelines are displayed and added to or modified as specific aspects are tested against other examples of the text type. Charts can be handed on to next year's teacher as a basis for further refinement using more complex texts. Only one text type is taught at any one time.

Modelling the Text Form	Intensive modelling is a powerful strategy used by teachers to reinforce and focus their pupils' understanding of the reading and writing of information texts. Teachers model the strategies and behaviours of an effective reader and writer by voicing their thoughts aloud as they read and write, e.g. *I need to write my recipe for making pancakes so that we can follow it today to make our pancakes. I know that when we write procedures I need to write my goal first, and then I need to list all the things we will need to make the pancakes...*

Modelling sessions should be brief and should not focus on too many elements.

When teachers model the reading and writing of a text form they refer to the purpose of the writing and the expected audience. They point out the language features of the form and show how they use the guidelines constructed with the pupils to help them write the text form. Detailed explanations of modelled reading and writing are provided in the *First Steps* book *Shared and Guided Reading and Writing, Key Stage 2*.

Reading Comprehension Activities	Reading comprehension activities that occur before and during reading are often taught and practised during the shared and guided reading component of the Literacy Hour. Activities that take place after reading can be used during the small group activity component of the Hour that follows.

Many of these activities are included in the short-term activities categorised as *before, during* and *after* activities. This categorisation helps teachers think about reading comprehension as a process, rather than a product.

<table>
<tr><td>

Shared and Guided Reading

</td><td>

Shared and guided reading enable a whole class or small group to join together as readers.

</td></tr>
</table>

Shared Reading

In shared reading sessions teachers introduce information books and indicate important features and conventions used in this type of text. They show pupils how knowledge of the structure and features of text types can help comprehension and how information texts differ from narratives.

Teachers talk about the audience and purpose for the text and the information the author needed to know before writing. They model how to find information, pointing out that information texts do not have to be read from cover to cover.

Over time, teachers and children talk about features such as the table of contents, index, glossary, headings and sub-headings, use of photographs and diagrams to support the text, the type of language used and the layout of the text.

Guided Reading

In guided reading children need their own copy of a text. Teachers and children discuss the topic of the text, linking it to the children's thoughts and experiences. During the introduction of a text, teachers initiate discussions on the title, illustrations and other text features, discussing how these assist in making meaning. Teachers then set questions that require the children to read to find answers. Children substantiate their answers from the text. Specific strategies being targeted are discussed in context. Detailed explanations of shared and guided reading are provided in the *First Steps* book *Shared and Guided Reading and Writing, Key Stage 2*.

<table>
<tr><td>

Shared and Guided Writing

</td><td>

Shared and guided writing provide opportunities for beginning readers and writers to practise and consolidate their understandings with teacher support.

</td></tr>
</table>

Shared Writing

Shared writing involves the class in:

- brainstorming ideas
- categorising information
- deciding what additional information is needed
- deciding on the appropriate text structure and the language features needed
- finding out information they will need
- devising a plan which may include headings and sub-headings if appropriate
- jointly writing the first draft
- jointly proof-reading, editing and revising the text.

Guided Writing

Guided writing provides children with the opportunity to write a new text form with support. Children brainstorm all the facts they know about a topic. The teacher writes the facts on cards that are then displayed on a board, overlapping words where children have duplicated facts.

Using the headings from the jointly constructed framework for the text form, the children sort the words under the appropriate headings. Depending on the children's level of expertise they can write a text, according to the jointly constructed framework for the form, in pairs, individually or with the teacher.

Guided writing allows pupils to progress at their own rate and gives the teacher the opportunity to work with pupils needing extra assistance. It is the natural sequel to shared writing and the precursor to independent writing. Detailed explanations of shared and guided writing are provided in the *First Steps* book *Shared and Guided Reading and Writing, Key Stage 2*.

Teaching Vocabulary and Sentence Structure

The component of the Literacy Hour that focuses on activities provides an excellent opportunity to teach children how to comprehend and compose the linguistic features of a particular text form.

For instance, if children are learning to read and write recounts, they need to understand fully the meaning of key words such as *who, when, where, what* and *why*. If a Literacy Hour has commenced with reading or writing as a shared experience, sentences from the text could be used to extend children's control over these text types by asking groups of children to invent, or choose from a given range, alternative beginnings or endings to sentence stems.

Independent Reading And Writing

Teachers can encourage children in Key Stage 2 to read and write on a daily basis by providing inviting book and writing areas. Below are some suggestions to consider when setting up these areas.

Book Corners

Book corners are comfortable places that entice children to sit and read. They may include cushions, bean bags or carpet for the children to sit or lie on. Posters featuring books, authors or topics are displayed where children can see them easily. The teacher can introduce these posters and their purpose and audience through discussion with the children.

Book corners display a selection of books including fiction and information texts. When choosing information texts, teachers ensure they provide a variety of text forms; for example, differing procedural texts, *Simple Cooking, Making Paper Aeroplanes*, or a class made instruction book, e.g. *How to Do Some Magic Tricks*, as well as reports on butterflies or transport and recent class-written recounts. Books are arranged attractively on bookshelves, on stands or in boxes. Books which teachers particularly want pupils to read are displayed so that children can see the covers.

When starting a class book corner, teachers begin with a small number of books and add to the collection, after reading and discussing new books on a daily basis. Some teachers like to store books they have read with children in a separate book box so that children know where to find their favourites. If big books have been shared with the class, it is sensible to have multiple copies in standard format because these titles will be sought by children for independent reading.

Provide access to books read to children and those used in guided reading sessions so that children can return to the texts as often as desired.

Writing Corners

Writing corners are places for children to practise their skills and understandings about writing in contexts that appeal to them. To entice children to write, teachers provide different colours and types of paper, small blank pads and books. A variety of writing implements, e.g. crayons, pencils, felt-tipped markers and pens, are also provided. Other stationery children enjoy using to enhance their writing are staplers, adhesive tape, glue, stamps and craft scissors. These stationery supplies can be stored in trays or boxes but they need to be easily accessed by the children. Teachers set instructions for using the writing corner with the children to minimise waste.

Frameworks, charts of language features and examples of writing are displayed where children are able to refer to them easily. Children's writing folders or books can be stored in boxes or crates where children can access them as they need to. Writing corners also include a notice board where children's work is displayed. The displayed work is changed regularly.

Computers are wonderful tools for young writers. Children have no fear of technology and are eager to use computers to achieve their goals. It is easy to teach pupils a few basic commands and gradually introduce them to a range of possibilities. Sometimes it is not even necessary to do that, as children are very good at teaching each other and quickly impart skills they may have acquired at home. If a computer can be set up as an adjunct to a writing area, children can jointly construct their own rules about turn-taking or sharing. Some teachers find that children work well in pairs.

Computers are not only motivating, but their flexibility can help children a great deal as they begin to feel the need to alter words or reconstitute sentences. Any writer knows how helpful it is to be able to change sentences or replace words that fail to do justice to the intended meaning. For young children, the ability to move words around is especially helpful, as it gives them a sense of control and makes them realise that words are the servants of a writer. Too often children feel that words on a page are immutable. They may feel trapped by their own composition, as if the words have taken control from them. Helping children to use a computer effectively can bring about a real breakthrough in this regard.

Children also like to be able to produce an impressive piece of writing. Although teachers stress that it is what writers say and how they say it that matters, children are only too aware of erratic print or many crossings out.

Sometimes it feels good to produce something that looks professional! At the same time it is important that children appreciate the value of the 'workings' of a piece of writing and that they know that adult writers also need to cross out or try out spellings. A computer-printed piece of writing should not be given greater value than a written one, but it can provide an additional impetus to a struggling young writer.

The use of the Internet can provide a wonderful range of purposes and audiences for young writers. Many schools have started to write to their counterparts in other parts of the world and send reports about their home community, descriptions of where they live and recounts of what they have been doing. The very real, live audiences with whom they are corresponding can motivate the most reluctant writers. They can also provide an interactive environment that helps children stand back from their own situation and realise that they need to provide a context for their writing. The immediacy and spontaneity of the Internet is invaluable.

Sharing and Reflecting

Sharing written work with others is a powerful teaching strategy because it makes writing meaningful and purposeful. Sharing new knowledge about books through book talks makes the sharer feel important and often motivates listeners to read a book.

Sharing and celebrating new knowledge is important as it encourages reflection and often suggests a future direction for learning. This occurs through questioning or by the provision of a simple structure such as the one suggested here which is used for book talks.

Sharing with the whole class is time-consuming and not all children who wish to share get the opportunity. It is important that all pupils are given the opportunity to share. Sharing need not necessarily be oral. Written work can be pinned up on the class 'Brag Board' or attached to the classroom door for parents and other passers-by to read.

Opportunities for sharing are organised on a daily basis. Teachers talk to children about the purposes of sharing their reading and writing. This encourages children to see sharing as an important part of the learning process.

Reflecting, unlike sharing, should focus not on what has been done, but on what has been learned. Reflection needs to be carefully modelled and taught. It is essential that, at the end of each session, children are able to reflect on whether they have achieved their target, or how much progress they have made towards it. Reflection should always be linked to the objective of the lesson, which is shared with children before teaching commences.

(Adapted from material written by Alison Dewsbury for the *First Steps* Project.)

Specific Strategies for Teaching Text Types

Teachers can set pupils up for successful reading and writing experiences by ensuring that the:

- subject matter is interesting and motivating

- purpose of the reading and writing is clear

- focus is on clear, concise comprehension and composition

- processes of reading and writing are reflective.

How to Select Strategies

Skilled readers and writers have at their disposal a number of metacognitive skills. These skills help them think about their own thinking – in this case the thinking processes that enable efficient and effective reading and writing. They know when to use a strategy, why a specific strategy should be used, and how the strategy is used. For example, a reader choosing a text knows that by skimming the text to gain a general impression or overview of the content, a decision could be made about whether the book is suitable for the reader's needs. The reader knows that this is a pre-reading strategy (when), that it is used to preview a text (why) and that the reading involves glancing at headings, sub-headings, layout and key vocabulary to get a sense of how useful the text will be (how). To encourage the development of these skills the following guidelines have been provided for strategy selection.

- Strategies chosen as part of a cohesive unit of work will be more useful than those chosen for isolated teaching.

- Strategies need to be explicitly taught at least four times before pupils can be expected to use them in a shared context.

- The when, why and how of a strategy is crucial. Pupils need to be able to recognise when a strategy can be used, why it should be used and how it should be used.

- Modelled, shared and guided reading and writing provide the ideal teaching contexts for moving pupils from the explicit teaching of a strategy through the supported use of a strategy to the independent use of a strategy. These teaching contexts are comprehensively explained in the *First Steps* book *Shared and Guided Reading and Writing, Key Stage 2*.

Before Reading and Writing Strategies

Before reading and writing strategies are designed to be brief and motivating, and to help pupils to do one or more of the following.

- Predict. Efficient readers are constantly making and revising predictions as they seek to make sense of text. They are asking questions like:

    – what do I already know?

    – what do I want and need to know?

    – what sort of text structure, layout and vocabulary do I expect to find in this book?

    – what strategies will I need to read this type of text?

    – what can I predict from the cover, title, contents list, illustrations, diagrams and photographs of this book?

  Skilled writers are constantly predicting how the intended audience for a piece of writing will react to the ideas, the structure and the vocabulary. They are asking questions like:

    – will the reader know that already?

    – what does the reader need to know?

    – will the reader follow that idea?

    – will the reader know what that word means?

- Set a purpose. Efficient readers know why they are reading and adjust their reading style to suit their purpose. They ask questions like:

    – why am I reading this – for enjoyment, retelling, information, to answer questions?

    – how shall I read this – should I skim, scan, read and re-read?

  Effective writers know why they are writing and adjust their writing style to suit their purposes. They ask questions like:

    – why am I writing this – to entertain, inform, inspire, or persuade?

    – how shall I write this – should I use paragraphs, dot points, first/third person?

Before Reading Strategies

Graphic Organiser

What is it?

The term graphic organiser is used in this book to describe a range of strategies that have in common the purpose of organising background knowledge for reading or writing. These strategies include semantic webs, concept maps, skeleton outlines, mind maps and structured overviews. While each strategy may have a claim to being unique in some way, what is common is the organisation of information into a framework that will assist comprehension or composition. Graphic organisers have been included as a pre-reading strategy here as a logical sequel to brainstorming. However, they are also powerful monitoring tools during and after reading and writing.

Why use it?

Graphic organisers encourage readers and writers to organise their background knowledge in preparation for the demands of comprehending and composing. For readers, this means predicting the concepts that may be introduced in the text, the way information might be presented in the text and the type of vocabulary that could be encountered. It is also an opportunity to refine the purpose of the reading by clarifying what is known and what the reader is keen to find out. For writers, the advance organiser is a tool to plan at a whole text level how ideas will be conveyed to the reader. It triggers the consideration of how ideas could be linked, cohesion maintained and which text type might be most appropriate.

Depending on when and how it is used, the graphic organiser could be considered a way of sorting brainstormed ideas, a way of organising predictions about a text, or even a note-making structure.

How do you use it?

Like brainstorming, the teaching of the graphic organiser can be conducted at a whole class, group or individual level, although explicit teaching of the strategy is most efficient at the whole class level.

Using the responses generated in a brainstorming session, pupils direct the teacher as to how the information should be categorised. The process is one of classifying and grouping related information. As a guide, information can be sorted in a logical, hierarchical way, with concepts leading to sub-concepts, as shown below. Ultimately, however, the framework can be determined by the users, that is, the pupils. Therefore agreement will need to be negotiated at a class and group level. Teachers would expect a greater degree of variation at the individual level.

Many diagrams lend themselves to the categorisation of ideas, and subsequently to the comprehension and composition of particular text types. A number of techniques can be used to strengthen the meaning of the graphic organiser. Question marks can symbolise doubt about the accuracy of information, dotted lines can show tenuous links, and the size of print and shape of enclosures can imply relationships between concepts. Colour can be used for similar effect.

Graphic organisers can be used during reading to monitor comprehension. For example, 'Our organiser shows what we knew about whales before we started reading... now that we are halfway through the text about whales, what would you add to or change on it?' Similarly, a graphic organiser used to plan a piece of non-fiction writing could be used to reflect on progress: 'If we look back at our plan, we were going to include a paragraph about the appearance of the whale, and so far we've written only about its location and behaviour.'

Graphic organisers are ideal tools for representing comprehension of a text and for making notes. By using an organisational framework which reflects the structure of the text, and entering key words to represent the relationship between ideas, pupils show that they understand the overall meaning of the text. Of course, explicit teaching and ongoing support will be necessary to provide pupils with the skills to recognise which frameworks most appropriately accommodate which sorts of information, but modelled, shared and guided reading and writing lessons are ideal forums for this teaching. The use of graphic organisers can be scaffolded by the teacher providing the framework and some of the major headings, or the framework alone. This approach is an effective means of supporting pupils, but can also be used as a means of assessment in some contexts. As an alternative to a list of questions, many teachers have found that asking pupils to complete a graphic organiser is a useful means of assessing their grasp of main ideas and relationships between them.

Each representation or diagram should be accompanied by a list of the signal words that will help pupils recognise relationships between ideas. Pupils need practice in identifying particular patterns in text and selecting appropriate methods of summarising the information.

Consider how these diagrams reflect links and relationships between ideas in information texts, and how the signal words alert the reader to the existence of a pattern.

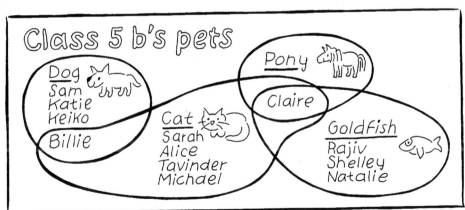

A Venn diagram can show the relationship between two or more (simply add more circles) ideas. Signal words associated with this comparison-contrast text pattern include: *although, whereas, yet, however, compared with, unlike, like, different, similar, on the other hand*. A table with two columns can also be used to compare two concepts, with the repetitive elements being the common factors. A single-column table can be used for text with a listing pattern. Signal words for a listing pattern include: *as well, in addition to, besides, furthermore, finally*.

A time line		About:	
Time	**Notes**		**Illustrations**

A timeline can show how events unfold over time. This time order pattern is normally signalled by: *after, next, before, firstly, secondly, finally.*

A flow chart can show how a set of instructions should be followed, particularly where an alternative course of action can be followed. Signal words used for this pattern are similar to those used for a timeline, with the addition of: *if... then, in the event.*

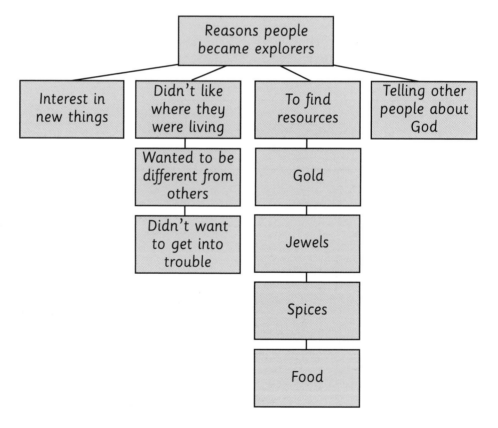

Tree diagrams can be adapted to represent two or more ideas by having a branch to house the supporting details of each one. The commonly used tree diagram with a single focus and numerous, but non-extended branches is ideal for representing the main idea and supporting details, either at a paragraph level, or at a whole text level. The sun diagram serves a similar purpose.

	Expensive to feed	Need to be exercised	Need grooming	Need home to be cleaned	Need affection
Dogs	✓ page 6	✓ page 6	✓ page 6		✓ page 6
Cats			✓ page 7		✓ page 8
Goldfish				✓ page 7	
Canaries				✓ page 9	✓ page 9
Horses	✓ page 5	✓ page 5	✓ page 5	✓ page 5	✓ page 5

A matrix, retrieval chart or semantic grid shows a comparison of a range of attributes of an object.

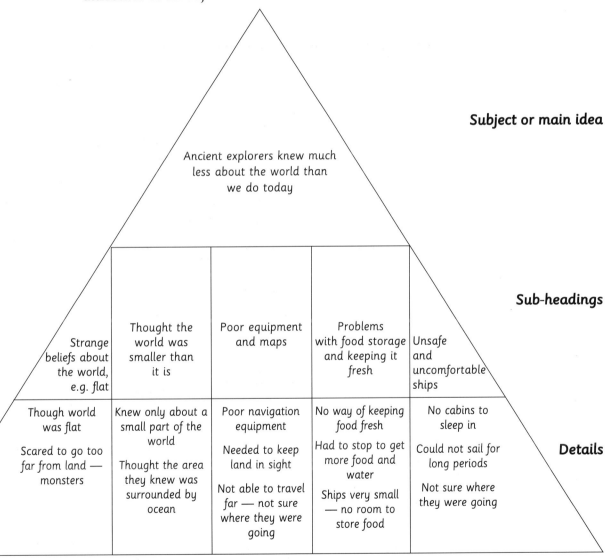

A pyramid can show the relationship of individual paragraphs to the main idea of a whole text, or can show the relationship of a cause to an effect or effects. Signal words include: *makes, causes, leads to, results in, so, consequently, so that, if, then, because.*

Before and After Charts

What is it?

Before and after charts are yet another way of organising brainstormed information. The chart can be used to record what is known about a topic before reading and after reading.

Why use it?

The 'before' section of these charts makes explicit what is known before reading and what needs to be discovered through reading. The 'after' sections provide a real purpose for reflecting on reading to find out what has been learned and what is yet to be learned.

How do you use it?

The before and after chart is best suited to a group or individual situation. When whole classes enter all they know about a topic in a before and after chart (unless they know very little) the chart becomes large and unwieldy.

After information about a topic is brainstormed, it is categorised and entered in the 'before' column headed *What we know about* _____. This information is in the form of key words or clauses and is entered under category headings. The question *What do I/we want to know about* _____? is then asked and the responses recorded in the appropriate column. After reading, all new information learned is entered in the 'after' column headed *What I/we have learned.* Any unanswered questions are entered in the final 'after' column headed *What we still need to learn* and can provide the motivation for further reading.

The following before and after chart is based on *Natural Disasters*, by Janeen Brian (Magic Bean, In-fact series).

Before Reading		After Reading	
What we know	**What we want to find out**	**What we learned**	**What we still want to know**
Types – earthquakes, cyclones, tidal waves, volcanoes	*Are famines and lightning strikes natural disasters?*	*Avalanches, floods, droughts and forest fires are also natural disasters. Famines are sort of caused by droughts. Lightning strikes can start fires.*	*Which natural disaster has killed the most people?*
Earthquakes – split the ground, measured on the Richter Scale	*What causes an earthquake?*	*Earthquakes are caused when plates of rock in the Earth's crust move against one another.*	*Can we predict earthquakes?*
Cyclones – happen lots in tropical areas	*Is a cyclone the same as a tornado and a typhoon?*	*A cyclone is called a hurricane or typhoon in some parts of the world.*	*Is a tornado the same as a hurricane, a typhoon and a cyclone?*
Tidal waves – wash away entire towns	*What causes tidal waves?*	*Tidal waves, or tsunamis, are caused by earthquakes under the ocean.*	
Volcanoes – cover towns in lava	*Where does lava come from?*	*Lava comes inside the Earth. It is like melted rock.*	*Can we predict volcanic eruptions?*

Skim Sheets

What is it?

The skim sheet strategy directs pupils to use chapter titles, headings and sub-headings to predict what information may be in a passage.

Why use it?

Skim sheets provide a means for the recording of predictions made through skimming. Skimming involves glancing through material to gain a general impression or overview of the content. This is the skill used by readers to quickly assess whether a text is going to meet their purpose.

How do you use it?

Skim sheets need explicit demonstration at a whole class level and can be supported at an individual level by pairing able with less able readers. Skimming is a skill that requires cumulative practice and experience with a range of texts to master.

Use a specific chapter or section of an information book that has headings and/or sub-headings. List the headings and sub-headings from the text on the skim sheet. Pupils skim read the section of text; that is, within a limited time they glance at the headings in the text with the intention of predicting what sort of information might be included. They work with partners to predict what information might be included in each section. Predictions are discussed and recorded on the skim sheet. Pupils read the text to assess the accuracy of their predictions, record the accuracy of their predictions and then make any necessary changes.

The simple skim sheet below is based on *Which is Which?* by Josephine Croser (Magic Bean, *In-fact* series).

Heading	**Information included**	**Information included, but inaccurate**	**Information not included**
Rabbit or hare? *Hares have longer ears.* *Hares have longer bodies.*	Yes	*Yes, hares are bigger.*	
Butterfly or moth? *Butterfly has coloured wings.* *Moths make cocoons.*	Yes.		*
Monkey or ape? *Monkeys have tails.* *Apes are bigger and stronger.*	Yes.		*

An adaptation of the skim sheet involves pupils skimming the headings, sub-headings or topic sentences listed on the skim sheet and turning them into questions. In doing this pupils are previewing the text layout and making predictions about what the main idea of each heading will be. To confirm or revise the prediction, pupils read each section and record their findings on the sheet. The discussion generated by this activity should focus on whether the detail of the paragraph answers the question posed as a main idea. The discussion is about how supporting detail can be summarised to generalise the main idea of a section of text, and how the topic sentence is often a clear signal as to the main idea of a paragraph.

The following skim sheet is based on two paragraphs from *The First Lunar Landing* by Rodney Martin (Magic Bean, *In-fact* series, page 6). The two paragraphs read:

> The astronauts thought some of the training was interesting. They travelled to different places and met the people who made their spacecraft. They spent hundreds of hours in a simulator, which was like a smart video game, where they could 'crash' their spacecraft without getting hurt.

> Sometimes they did not enjoy the training. One reason was they were often away from their families. Another reason was some of the training was very uncomfortable. For example, they disliked being spun around in a huge machine like the gravitron at an amusement park. They nicknamed this machine 'the wheel'.

Skim Sheet Adaptation

Topic sentence	After skimming. What question does the paragraph answer?	After reading and discussion. What question does the paragraph answer?
The astronauts thought some of the training was interesting.	*Did the astronauts think the training was interesting?*	*What was interesting about the training?*
Sometimes they did not enjoy the training.	*What did the astronauts not enjoy about the training?*	*What did the astronauts not enjoy about the training?*

Anticipation Guide

What is it?

The anticipation guide consists of a series of statements that reflect common misconceptions about a topic. Prior to reading, pupils use their existing knowledge to categorise each statement as either true or false.

Why use it?

Anticipation guides encourage pupils to consider carefully what they already know about a topic, create a specific purpose for reading and provide an opportunity to practise scanning skills. Scanning is reading quickly, but selectively, to locate a specific detail such as a name, date or place.

How do you use it?

Anticipation guides can be used by pupils independently, although the discussion about where a specific detail was found and how it confirms or rejects a listed statement is extremely valuable. The skill of scanning by using contents pages, indexes, headings, sub-headings, topic sentences and key words will need to be taught explicitly in a modelled or shared reading setting.

From a text, draw statements that reflect misconceptions or appear unlikely, but that can be confirmed or rejected by the text. Write the statements on the anticipation guide in the order in which they appear in the text. Pupils read the statements alone and mark them true or false, then they scan the text looking for the specific reference to the statement, and reject or confirm their previous prediction. They record a page and line reference to substantiate their claims.

The following anticipation guide is based on *Natural Disasters*, by Janeen Brian (Magic Bean, *In-fact* series)

Statement	What I think	What the book says	Page and line reference
Lava and thick ash from volcanoes can burn or bury entire towns.	*True*	*True*	*page 4, under picture*
Cockroaches know when an earthquake is coming.	*False*	*True*	*page 7, in grey box*
Cyclones can twist people's mouths so they can't speak.	*False*	*True*	*page 9, in grey box*
Most people who die in fires die from burns.	*True*	*False*	*page 16, in grey box*

Before Writing Strategies

Text Reconstruction

What is it?

Text reconstruction is the reassembling of any fragmented whole text.

Why use it?

The value of reconstructing text is in pupils becoming aware of the structure and cohesive devices of a text type, and verbalising how knowledge of these features enabled them to put the text together again.

How do you use it?

Pupils are given an instructional text that has been cut into pieces, as shown below. They are encouraged to use the main idea of each piece of text (often a paragraph), linking words and phrases to establish the sequence of events.

The following steps are implemented.

Replace the back cover of the calculator.

When the calculator fails to show a lighted display or does not compute correctly, the batteries are run down and must be replaced. The following procedure will result in the correct installation of new batteries.

Remove the old batteries and replace with the new batteries.

Turn the calculator on and test the display and the accuracy of the computation.

Take off the back cover.

Insert and tighten the two screws.

Replacement of Batteries in the XYZ Calculator

In order to complete the battery installation, a small Phillips screwdriver is required. Two new AAA size batteries should be used.

Undo the two screws in the back of the calculator.

Text reconstruction activities are most useful with text types with a distinct sequence of paragraphs. However, where the sequence is not prescriptive, excellent discussion can arise as pupils generate reasons to justify why their order of elements is effective. For example, pupils may argue that a report reads better with details about location first and description of appearance later. There will not always be one solution, but the discussion will focus on crucial links in meaning. Furthermore, pupils will become aware that the frameworks are open to manipulation.

Text Completion

What is it?

Text completion is a variation of text reconstruction. Pupils who have been exposed to a particular text type through modelled and shared reading are given a text that has a distinct section (a paragraph or a stage) missing. The pupils must decide which paragraph is missing and complete it.

Why use it?

Text completion encourages pupils to consider all the essential components of a text type and how they work together to achieve a purpose. An explanation missing a paragraph about definition will be recognisable to pupils who have seen and worked with the explanation framework.

How do you use it?

Delete a key paragraph or component from a text and ask pupils to read the text and suggest what is missing. Upon identification of the missing element, ask pupils to work in pairs or groups to write the missing component.

At the paragraph level, using the lead from a newspaper report, teachers can explain that a necessary element from the *who, when, where* and *why* details has been omitted. In each instance, the text used must be immediately recognisable as lacking an element because many elements at a whole text level or paragraph level are optional.

Oral Presentation

What is it?

Oral presentation is the name given to the range of contexts in which pupils have an opportunity to present an oral version of a text form.

Why use it?

Oral presentations provide opportunities for pupils to become familiar with a text structure in a broad, non-threatening manner. Oral language is less permanent than writing and open to more rapid adjustment and feedback.

How do you use it?

The following examples illustrate a range of ways in which oral presentation can be used.

- A pupil brings a toy to school and, during a newstelling session, explains how the toy works.

- During time provided for reflection, pupils share the procedure they followed to test a hypothesis in science.

- As preparation for an art lesson, pupils are asked to visualise a specific object – its shape, colours and texture – and describe it to their partner.

During oral presentation, teachers can use questions to guide pupils, and where appropriate make references to pupil-constructed charts around the room. For example, a child having problems sequencing the steps of a procedure would be asked, 'What was the first thing you had to do? What did you do after that?'

Positive comments about children's efforts will help them focus on improving their understanding of the attributes of a given text form. For example, 'I like the way Kirpal told us all the steps in order.'

It is important to remember that oral language is not open to the same reflection and revision as written language, and will not be as precise or specific. Pupils may require time for rehearsal, or may choose to use objects and/or notes or frameworks to assist them.

Although oral presentation is predominantly used as an activity leading up to the writing of a text form, it has similar worth as an activity to consolidate understandings during joint construction and independent writing of a form.

Drawing

What is it?

Drawing in this sense refers to the use of diagrams and symbols to convey relationships such as sequence, chronological order, and cause and effect.

Why use it?

Drawing can provide a useful bridge from the abstract oral form to the demands of the written form. Reluctant and struggling writers are able to clarify their thoughts by drawing pictures or diagrams to represent, for instance, each step in a procedure, or the sequence of events that make up the cause-effect paragraph of an explanation. Similarly, drawing a particular animal or object will allow the artist to reflect on the attributes of the subject, making a written description less daunting.

How do you use it?

Encourage pupils to draw pictures to represent key ideas as part of their planning before writing a first draft. In the case of explanations, instructions and reports, the more deliberate drawing of diagrams and illustrations that will accompany the text in publication will help pupils clarify the attributes, relationships and processes that need to be described in words.

Collecting, Analysing and Displaying

What is it?

Collecting, analysing and displaying are the ongoing processes stimulated by a focus on a text type. Once pupils have established what a text type looks like, what it is used for and where it is generally found, a search for examples to analyse and display can begin.

Why use it?

Pupils need to see how text types are used to achieve social purposes and the wide number of ways in which those purposes are achieved.

How do you use it?

Having seen a particular text form in a shared reading session, pupils can be encouraged to scan books, magazines, etc, in search of examples of the form. Copies of the form can be displayed and discussion developed about similarities and differences. A variety of examples provides a strong foundation for discussion in which the pupils problem-solve the features of a text form. Problem-solving samples are generally all examples of one type of text form, and can sometimes be unrepresentative. For example, four recipes may not reflect the diversity of a range of procedures. Procedures from a range of contexts, with a range of purposes and audiences, provide pupils with opportunities to see how language features are adapted to suit different situations.

Direct Modelling

What is it?

Direct modelling is the process of analysing each paragraph or meaningful unit of a text by asking what its purpose is. Once the purpose is established, pupils are asked to suggest a label for that part of the framework of the text form. The label is intended to reflect the paragraph's purpose. The framework suggested by the pupils may be crude in the first instance. However, this will highlight their degree of understanding and provide a basis for further work. With each reference to the framework, the framework should become more accurate.

Why use it?

Direct modelling enhances text level comprehension by teaching pupils to reflect on the purpose of parts of text. It also clarifies the role of key elements in text type frameworks.

How do you use it?

In simple terms the dialogue is built upon the following scaffold.

Teacher: *What is the purpose of this heading?*
Pupil: *It tells the reader what the instructions are for.*
Teacher: *What can we call it?*
Pupil: *The title.*
Teacher: *What is the purpose of this first paragraph?*
Pupil: *To tell what is to be done.*
Teacher: *What can we call it?*
Pupil: *Aim or goal.*
Teacher: *What is the purpose of this list?*
Pupil: *It explains what we need to do the job.*
Teacher: *What would be a good label for that part?*
Pupil: *Requirements.*
Teacher: *What is the purpose of this part?*
Pupil: *It's a list of steps to take to do the job.*
Teacher: *Can you suggest a label for that part?*
Pupil: *The method.*
Teacher: *What is the purpose of the conclusion?*
Pupil: *How to test it to see if it works.*
Teacher: *What could we call it?*
Pupil: *Evaluation.*

Pupils from a Year 5 class gave these labels to paragraphs of an Explanation.

I think
Why I think
Why I think
Why I think
Why I'm right

While the labels given to each paragraph of the text type may lack formality, the pupils have successfully grasped the basic framework of thesis, arguments and summary (including reassertion of the thesis).

Brainstorming

What is it?

A simple but essential way of preparing for reading or writing, brainstorming is the rapid collection of ideas without discussion or evaluation.

Why use it?

Brainstorming enables pupils to see the importance of background knowledge to comprehension and composition. It is perhaps the simplest of reflective processes, yet one of the most powerful. By establishing what is known, pupils gain direction when reading (to find out what is important to them) and when writing (to marshal thoughts into manageable units like paragraphs).

How do you use it?

Brainstorming can be conducted at a whole class, group or individual level, although explicit teaching of the strategy is most efficient at the whole class level.

The generic question 'What do you already know about this topic?' is asked and responses are recorded. This can be done verbally, by the teacher recording pupil responses on a board, or in a written mode, by responses being recorded on pieces of card. Card allows ideas to be moved and categorised at a later time.

Responses are clipped – that is, what is recorded consists of keywords or clauses, not extended sentences. Where verbal responses are long or unwieldy, it is more productive for the teacher to ask, 'How would you sum that up in a few key words?' rather than writing a personal interpretation of the main idea of the response.

No discussion or evaluation of ideas occurs. If, in response to the question, 'What do we know about whales?' a pupil offers that they are fish, the brainstorming session is not the time or place to dismiss the idea. The opportunity to question the accuracy of information arises in the actual reading or preparation for writing.

<table>
<tr><td>

During Reading and Writing Strategies

</td><td>

During reading and writing strategies are designed to be brief and help pupils to self-monitor and adjust what they are doing. Competent readers and writers are constantly asking themselves questions like:

</td></tr>
</table>

- What was my purpose in reading or writing this?

- Am I making sense?

- Where did I not make sense?

- Is this information worth remembering (reading) or including (writing)?

- What strategies can I use to tackle this part – re-reading, reading on (reading) or rewriting, changing key words (writing)?

- What is being stated (or what am I stating) at a literal level, inferential level and evaluative level?

- What does that word mean (reading) or what word best expresses that thought (writing)?

During reading and writing strategies are generally most effective within the context of modelled, shared and guided reading and writing. Reflecting on the making of meaning, what strategies are being used and how to deal with difficult words are the processes addressed within these contexts. These strategies are employed by tackling the text in stages. At the completion of a stage – that is, a break in the reading or writing of a text predetermined by the teacher – pupils are asked to reflect, clarify, question, summarise and set a new direction for the next stage. These are the elements of effective self-monitoring. The following strategies are intended for implementation in this way.

During Reading Strategies

Difficult Words Chart

What is it?

The difficult words chart is a method for clarifying new or unknown vocabulary in a non-fiction text.

Why use it?

The chart helps pupils use context clues to work out word meanings. In doing so, pupils are required to paraphrase, which enhances note-making and summarising skills.

How do you use it?

Difficult words charts can be used before, during or after reading. By using a class or group difficult words chart, tough vocabulary can be defined as the text is read which will enhance during reading comprehension.

During shared or guided reading, have an enlarged copy of the difficult words chart nearby. After reading a section of text, ask a pupil to summarise what the section was about, and ask if the text included any words they weren't sure about. If no response is given, use a prompt (*What about that word* molten; *does anyone know what that means?*). Enter any word offered in the word column, list the page on which it is found and ask pupils to find context clues that might suggest a meaning for the word. Record any context clues in the appropriate column. Ask for and record pupils' explanation of the word meaning. If necessary, check and record a glossary or dictionary definition.

The following difficult words chart is based on *Natural Disasters*, by Janeen Brian (Magic Bean, *In-fact* series).

Word	Page	Context clues	Our explanation	Dictionary definition
molten	4	*hot lava, magma*	*melted rock*	*liquefied by great heat*
topple	7		*knock over*	*cause to tumble or fall headlong*
tsunamis	7	*Page 13, giant waves caused by earthquakes*	*giant waves*	
evaporate	14	*water turns into water vapour*	*water turns into a gas*	*turn into vapour*

Main Idea Pyramid

What is it?

The main idea pyramid is strategy for organising and recording details to establish the main idea of paragraphs and, if necessary, an entire text.

Why use it?

The main idea pyramid shows one way of deciding upon a main idea for a piece of text. The pyramid shows clearly the relationship between supporting detail and the main idea.

How do you use it?

Main idea pyramids require repeated demonstration and explicit teaching before pupils can be expected to use them independently.

During shared or guided reading, ask the children to close their book(s) and brainstorm all that they can remember from a selected paragraph. Record the details that they recall at the base of the pyramid. Any doubtful information can be substantiated by referring back to the paragraph. Discuss, given the information that has been recalled, what the paragraph could be called (i.e. the main idea).

By following a similar process for further paragraphs, a collection of main ideas can be assembled on the second level of the pyramid. If appropriate, a main idea for the entire text can be determined and recorded at the apex of the pyramid.

Reading for the main idea can be difficult for some children. The task can be scaffolded by offering a choice of two or three main ideas, and having pupils choose the most appropriate one.

The main idea pyramid below is based on *The First Lunar Landing* by Rodney Martin (Magic Bean, *In-fact* series, page 13). The paragraph selected reads:

> Armstrong and Aldrin worked on the moon for two hours and twenty minutes. Some of their jobs were to:
>
> - collect moon rocks and soil samples;
>
> - set up a machine to measure moonquakes;
>
> - set up an experiment to study the sun's rays;
>
> - set up a mirror so a laser beam sent from Earth could measure the distance between Earth and the moon.

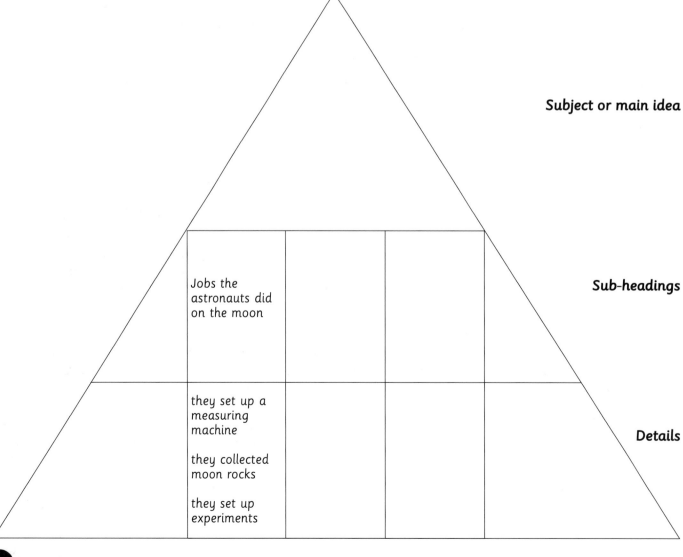

Subject or main idea

Jobs the astronauts did on the moon

Sub-headings

they set up a measuring machine

they collected moon rocks

they set up experiments

Details

The paragraph that was selected here provided scaffolding for pupils because details were listed, and therefore were easier to recall. Although few paragraphs feature a bulleted point format like this one, it is useful to select paragraphs with clear topic sentences and simple listing patterns when introducing this strategy to pupils.

Pyramids using a more difficult main idea can be constructed by asking pupils to listen to or read a text made up of several paragraphs. The children then write the details they can recall on cards, one detail per card. The cards must be categorised into paragraphs at the bottom level of the pyramid before the main idea of each paragraph can be determined and recorded in the second level of the pyramid.

Reading Guide

What is it?

The reading guide is a set of written directions and questions intended to guide pupils through the independent reading of an information text. Reading guides can be thought of as combining the direction of a guided reading session and the enjoyment of a treasure hunt.

Why use it?

When children begin to read independently, many still require support in monitoring their reading. Reading guides assist comprehension by:

- highlighting significant ideas and the relationships between them

- indicating sections that are peripheral or irrelevant and can be skimmed

- stimulating thinking about key ideas

- reinforcing the importance of regular monitoring of comprehension (summarising, questioning, locating troublesome vocabulary).

How do you use it?

Reading guides are written for information texts that will be used on a regular basis. They can be designed to meet the needs of readers who have different abilities, but should also be able to be used independently. Modelling of their use and shared practice will increase the likelihood of pupils being able to work independently and effectively.

To design a reading guide:

- determine the overall purpose for reading – this need not be a curriculum content objective and may simply involve reading for information;

- select sections of the text that are most important to achieving the purpose;

- plot a path through the text by directing pupils to sections of text, posing questions, requesting predictions and prompting summaries.

The following reading guide is based on *The First Lunar Landing* by Rodney Martin (Magic Bean, *In-fact* series). The curriculum focus is History Study Unit 3b – changes in industry and transport, including the impact of new technologies, e.g. motor cars, computers, space travel. The objective is for pupils to develop the skills of prediction and confirmation.

Reading directions	Task
Read the introduction to the book on page 3.	Look at the Contents page opposite. The next page, page 4, is about the Apollo Spacecraft and the Saturn V Rocket. Quickly draw what you think the rocket might look like. How tall do you think it might have been? (*30 metres*) Put an X in your drawing where you think the astronauts might sit.
Read page 4 and look carefully at the diagram.	How tall was the rocket? (*11 metres*) Were you right about where the astronauts sat? You can see the astronauts on the opposite page. Page 6 is about their training for the journey. What sort of training do you think they would need to do? (*Dizziness training, coping with gravity, practice at eating, how to use the communications equipment*)
Read page 7.	Tick the training needs you predicted that were listed on page 6. The next two pages are about the journey. How long do you think it might have taken them to get to the moon and back? (*4 days*) What would they do during a day in space? (*Eat, communicate with base, check their directions*)
Read pages 8 and 9.	How long did the astronauts expect that it would take them to get to the moon and back? (*8 days*) Tick the things you predicted they would do in space that were included on page 9. Pages 10, 11 and 12 are about the journey and landing on the moon. Before you skim these pages, predict what sort of work the astronauts might do once they were on the moon. (*Collect rocks, make maps, set up communications equipment, look for any sign of life*)
Skim pages 10, 11 and 12. Read page 13.	Tick the parts of your prediction that were correct. Close the book and write down the main ideas that you can recall from your reading today. (*The rocket was 11 metres tall and had a module at the top where the astronauts sat. The astronauts had to learn how to do lots of things before they left – like coping with gravity and using special equipment. In space astronauts ate, communicated with base, slept, relaxed and checked that they were still on course. On the moon they collected rocks and set up experiments.*)

<table>
<tr><td>

During Writing Strategies

Sentence Manipulation

</td></tr>
</table>

What is it?

Sentence manipulation is the rearrangement of words, phrases and clauses to enhance meaning.

Why use it?

Sentence manipulation is the key way in which authors make meaning clearer and more effective. Variation in sentence length and in sentence beginnings, for example, can maintain a reader's interest and give impact to information. Research has indicated that sentence manipulation plays a large part in the development of writers. Many children battle first with the concept of a sentence, and then with the control of its obvious flexibility. Time spent on sentence manipulation activities, all of which are easily linked to a writing focus, is invaluable to the developing writer. Shared literature, individual writing excerpts and text from newstelling provide an authentic context for these activities.

How do you use it?

Sentence-makers

Sentence-makers have the infinite potential of the sentence itself. A simple holding strip and a handful of word cards can lead to a range of activities that can be conducted on a class, group or individual basis. For example:

- Basic sentence-making: allow the children to construct sentences at will, using news sessions and exciting events, favourite books and word banks to stimulate their choice of words.

- Sentence expansion: use the sentence-maker to extend existing sentences by inserting additional adjectives, phrases and clauses.

- Sentence reduction: use the sentence-maker to reduce a long sentence to its simplest form by removing one word at a time. This activity is much more difficult than the preceding one as the sentence must be re-read each time to see if it still makes sense. It is important to recognise that beginning writers usually need to add relevant information while more advanced authors benefit from the reduction or tightening of sentences.

- Sentence transformation: use the sentence-maker to transform a sentence by taking turns to change one word at a time. A noun must be changed for a noun, a verb for a verb, and so on. Decide whether nonsense will be allowed.

Most | surfers | are | good | swimmers | .

Most | surfers | are | poor | swimmers | .

Most | surfers | are | poor | talkers | .

- Matching sentence parts: copy a series of sentences from a popular story or book onto card strips. Cut the strips into individual word cards and mix them up. Have the children match them up to make either sense or nonsense.

wall | Humpty | a | . | All | men | great | Humpty | sat

Humpty | on | had | the | king's | . | fall | a | Dumpty

horses | the | all | Humpty | couldn't | again | and | King's | together | .

- Sentence completion: make a series of sentence beginnings or sentence endings and let the children invent the missing part. This activity takes on extra importance when conjunctions are used.

Our | class | will | go | camping | if

John | knocked | on | the | door | but

unless | they | take | their | umbrellas | .

although | they | felt | very | sick | .

- Sentence modelling: use a familiar sentence pattern from a shared text as the basis for the construction of more sentences.

- Sentence comparison: by rewriting the text using the children's own language and discussing the two (or more) different forms, the teacher provides a focus point for discussion of how word order affects meaning and how sentences may be rearranged to become more appealing.

' | No | , | no | , | no | , | ' | said | the | village | monkey | loudly | .

' | No | , | no | , | no | , | ' | said | the | town | ranger | loudly | .

the | town | ranger | said | ' | No | , | no | , | no | , | ' | loudly | .

- Sentence transformation – singular to plural (or vice versa): discuss the changes necessary when the subject of the sentence becomes plural.

Victor | is | going | to | the | Royal | Show | on | Sunday | .

The | Johnson | twins | are | going | to | the | Royal | Show | on | Saturday | .

- Sentence transformation (tenses): compare the construction of the sentence in the three main tenses.

Present

| I | | am | | catching | | tadpoles | | . |

Past

| I | | caught | | tadpoles | | . |

Future

| I | | shall | | be | | catching | | tadpoles | | next | | week | | . |

- Sentence stems: manipulate sentence structure to enhance the meaning of the sentence stem provided.

| It's | | good | | when |

| It's | | great | | when |

| It's | | terrific | | when |

Chain writing

Chain writing is the name given to the gradual expansion of a sentence.

- Select a word related to the theme you are developing, e.g. spiders.

- Ask the children to suggest words that describe spiders, e.g.

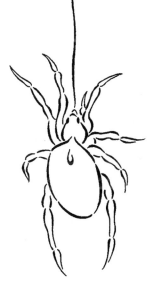

hairy
scary
black
sneaky   *spiders*
horrible
long-legged

- Then ask what spiders do and add the words to the list, e.g.

hairy   *climb*
scary   *hide*
black   *lurk*
sneaky   *spiders*   *creep*
horrible   *bite*
long-legged   *sleep*

- Now combine the words to make sentences, e.g.

Hairy spiders creep
Black spiders hide.
Horrible spiders bite.

- Next list where spiders do things and add these to the list, e.g.

hairy		*climb*	*in the garden*
scary		*hide*	*in the bathroom*
black		*lurk*	*under the wood pile*
sneaky	*spiders*	*creep*	*inside the lampshade*
horrible		*bite*	*in their webs*
long-legged		*sleep*	*on the pergola*

- Combine these as before to make different sentences, e.g.

  Long-legged spiders sleep in the bathroom.
  Scary spiders lurk inside the lampshade.

- Other questions can be asked to elicit additional responses, e.g.

When?
at night
during the day
just before dawn
every day
once a week

Why?
to find food
just for fun
to find a friend
to stay warm
because it's a habit

- Sentences can be written on coloured card and made into books.

- Children can be asked to write their own texts about spiders now that they have a wide range of ideas and words to stimulate their imaginations.

Physical sentence reconstruction
The obvious extension of chain writing and sentence-making is to list words and phrases on individual cards and use them for sentence creation and reconstruction. This is best achieved by asking individual children to be responsible for one card each. As a group, the children involved must arrange themselves in an order that makes sense. The advantages of this exercise are that:

- a large number of children become involved

- weaker children find assistance in the guidance of their classmates

- children start to realise the relationships between words (for example, *In every sentence we make, Martin, who has the word 'hairy', stands on the left-hand side of Ricky, who has the word 'spider'*)

- judgements can be made about the most appropriate sentence for the context, e.g.

  Which sentence fits best?

  Hairy spiders creep in the garden every day.

  or

  Every day hairy spiders creep in the garden.

  or

  In the garden hairy spiders creep every day.

  or

  In the garden every day hairy spiders creep.

<table>
<tr><td>Sentence Diagrams</td><td>Sentence manipulation need not always be a formal activity. The conversation below could be part of a one-to-one conference, a group conference or a class focus on sentence expansion:</td></tr>
</table>

Teacher:	*Who went to the pool, Bruce?*
Bruce:	*Shelley and I.*
Teacher:	*How could you add that to your recount?*
Bruce:	*Shelley and I went to the pool.*
Teacher:	*Well done, Bruce! How did you get to the pool?*
Bruce:	*We walked.*
Teacher:	*How could we include that part in your sentence?*
Bruce:	*Shelley and I walked to the pool.*
Teacher:	*Why did you go to the pool, Bruce?*
Bruce:	*Because it was hot at home.*
Teacher:	*Could that be added to your sentence?*
Bruce:	*Shelley and I walked to the pool because it was hot at home.*

We can show these changes, including transformations, reductions, expansions and rearrangements, in a diagram.

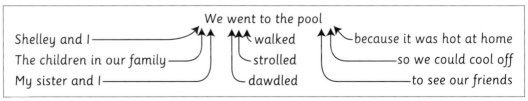

Note-making

What is it?

Note-making is the recording of key words in a text, usually nouns or verbs, as a means of identifying and extracting important information from texts.

Why use it?

Note-making allows a reader to recall extended and dense text, organise and summarise comprehended information, and record information for later use. It enhances a reader's ability to recall significant concepts and the relationships between them in a text.

How do you use it?

Note-making is a sophisticated skill and needs to be taught explicitly to pupils in modelled, shared and guided reading and writing sessions. Teaching the strategy of note-making will consist of explicit modelling, followed by a scaffolded opportunity to apply the demonstrated skill and reflective discussion about what was effective. The use of pairs and groups to generate key words is an excellent way of sharing why some words are chosen and others are not. When pupils display a readiness for independent note-making, the text used must be matched to the reading ability of the pupil or group of pupils.

The following guidelines provide a process that can be used to teach note-making skills in a motivating, purposeful and supportive context. Each lesson should begin with a review of the purpose of making notes:

- to help recall

- to record for another purpose like an assignment or project

- to help organise and summarise thoughts.

Picture stimulus
- Ask pupils to examine a large picture depicting a topical focus. For example, if the science focus is spiders, present a large photo of a spider.

- Discuss the picture, clarifying any vocabulary pupils are unsure of *(Yes, those funny eyes are called compound eyes)*.

- Ask pupils to write four or five individual words that would remind them of the picture. Explain that these words will generally be nouns *(legs)*, verbs *(climbs)* or adjectives *(hairy)*, and that words like *it, the,* and *has* don't aid the recall of anything in the picture. Explain how some key words need to be associated with others because they can't carry meaning alone e.g. *eight legs*.

- Share key words recorded by the children and talk about how effective they are in recalling the picture.

- Ask pupils to put one or more of the key words in a sentence about the picture.

- Share the sentences and discuss how key words have helped summarise the picture.

Picture stimulus and simple associated text
- Ask pupils to examine a large picture and read aloud a simple descriptive paragraph.

- Ask pupils to select four or five key words from the paragraph that would help them recall the paragraph and the picture. If possible, the children should each have a copy of the paragraph so that key words can be circled, underlined or highlighted.

- Share the key words selected and discuss their worth.

- Ask pupils to use the key words to write a sentence about the picture and paragraph.

Simple text
- Ask pupils to read aloud a simple descriptive paragraph.

- Ask them to select four or five key words from the paragraph that would help them recall the main idea. If possible, they should each have a copy of the paragraph so that key words can be circled, underlined or highlighted.

- Share the key words selected and discuss their worth. Begin by finding the key words common to most individuals or groups of children. Where words serve a similar purpose, ask the pupils to judge which word carries more meaning. For example, 'Jillian has the key word *many* to accompany the key word *legs*. Alison has the word *eight* to accompany the word *legs*. Which word tells us more about a spider's legs?'

- Ask pupils to use the key words to write a sentence about the paragraph.

Selecting from extended text
- Present pupils with a descriptive text about three paragraphs long. The paragraphs should have distinct main ideas marked by either sub-headings or topic sentences. For example, an extended text on spiders could have one paragraph headed *What spiders eat*, one headed *Where spiders live* and a third headed *What spiders do*.

- Ask the children to select a nominated number of key words to answer the question *Where do spiders live?* The number of key words should be adjusted to reflect the density of ideas in the text.

- Share which paragraph was chosen as the source of the key words. Explain the importance of using sub-headings and/or topic sentences to ignore some information in pursuit of more important information.

- Discuss the key words selected.

- Put the key words in a sentence (or two) which summarises the paragraph.

Selecting from a complete text
- Ask pupils to choose one question from a list designed to be answered within a selected text. For example, *What do spiders eat? Why are spiders useful? How do spiders make webs? How do spiders reproduce?*

- Provide the children with the text about spiders and model how, using an example question as a starting point, a reader could use the contents page, index, chapter headings, sub-headings and topic sentences to find the information required in the text.

- Ask them to follow the demonstration, locate the information and select the key words necessary to answer the question.

- Ask pupils to use the key words to write a sentence or two that answers the question.

- A table like the one below may be useful in guiding the process.

Topic: Spiders Question: What do spiders look like?	
Key words	**Sentence answers**
many types *2 body parts* *8 legs* *compound eyes*	*There are many different types of spiders, but all have two body parts, eight legs and compound eyes.*

Generating a question
- Provide pupils with a text that is motivating and interesting.

- Ask pupils to skim the contents page and pose a question that provides a purpose for reading. (*What would you like to know about this topic that this text could answer?*)

- The children then use the contents page, index, chapter headings, sub-headings and topic sentences to find the information required in the text.

- Ask pupils to locate the information and select the key words necessary to answer the question.

- Ask them to use the key words to write a sentence or two that answers the question.

- Provide an opportunity for pupils to share their findings.

After Reading and Writing Strategies

After reading and writing strategies are designed to help pupils to:

- reflect and respond to text; after reading and writing, competent readers and writers ask themselves questions like:

  - did I achieve my purpose in reading or writing this?

  - did I understand what I read (did my reader understand what I wrote)?

  - how does this text read (or written) now make me feel?

  - what did I understand (or express) at a literal level, inferential level and evaluative level?

- select, organise and use information for a specific purpose; after reading, competent readers and writers ask themselves questions like:

  - what do I do with this text (read or written) now?

  - what information is critical?

  - how can I recall this text if necessary – what summary of text structure will enable me to remember key parts of the text?

After reading strategies have the advantage of being open-ended, especially where they are individualised. Where pre-reading strategies must be brief, and during reading strategies are wedged in between shared and guided reading of a text, after reading strategies afford greater flexibility in terms of time and method. However, this flexibility has long been the bane of their effectiveness, as reproduced activity sheets have become ends in themselves. Clearly, for after reading strategies to be worthwhile they must be purposeful and encourage the application of taught skills.

After Reading Strategies

What is it?

Cloze procedure is the omission of single words or groups of words from text for the purpose of testing or teaching comprehension.

Cloze Procedure

Why use it?

Cloze can be manipulated to provide practice in the use of syntactic, semantic and graphophonic cues. Pupils can be taught to use their knowledge of language structures, the context of the sentence or text and the initial, medial or final letters to identify missing words.

How do you use it?

There are several varieties of cloze. Each can be configured to achieve a different purpose. For example, *a cloze p_____ that leaves initial letters encourages the use of initial l_____ as a cue to word identification.* What is most important in the use of cloze when teaching the comprehension of information texts is that the cloze procedure is used to teach reading skills rather than test knowledge. Compare the following cloze passages.

	Cloze test	Cloze exercise
Example	Pyramid of Cheops A few facts about the Pyramid of Cheops. 1 It is made out of _____ blocks. 2 These blocks are made of _____.	Pyramid of Cheops A few facts about the Pyramid of _____. 1 It is made out of 2,300,000 _____. 2 These blocks are ____ of limestone.
Features	Relies on the recall of previously encountered information.	Provides context clues to help pupils decide on the deleted words.
Purpose	• Test of pupil knowledge • Test of reading ability	• Exercise to teach the use of context clues

Deleting words directly from a piece of text read recently tends to encourage recall of literal details, in a way similar to a memory test. One very effective way of focusing cloze exercises on comprehension is to write a summary of a piece of information text to be read by pupils. Delete selected words which carry meaning and ask pupils to complete the passage.

The way in which the cloze passage is completed also affects its worth as a reading comprehension strategy. When pupils have an opportunity to substantiate their choice of word – and any reasonable choice is accepted – cloze becomes an exercise in reading and thinking. Pupils should be encouraged to generate their own answers, but then to discuss them and revise them on the basis of what sounds right. It is useful to stage cloze exercises so the discussion takes place after a section of text. This prevents weaker readers being misled by inappropriate selections early in the text. So the lesson would incorporate teacher modelling, individual attempts at the words missing in a paragraph, discussion with a peer or group, revision of answers and reading of the next paragraph to continue the cycle. Teacher input to discussion at a group level, or later at a whole class level, should focus on how the reader was able to choose an appropriate word for the space. Discussion centres on the context clues that were used to decide upon a logical word, and where the text is enlarged, arrows and colour might be used to highlight their role in completing that part of the cloze.

Transforming

What is it?

Transforming is the label given to the process of using the content of one text form in another. For example, the story of Cinderella could be written as a newspaper report with the headline, *Mystery Woman at Palace Ball*.

Why use it?

The value of transforming is in the need for pupils to select relevant detail, and reshape the main ideas of the text in a different form. In doing so, pupils are using note-making skills with a specific purpose in mind.

How do you use it?

Explicit modelling and support is necessary to teach transformation. Note-making skills must be sufficiently developed to draw facts from fictional texts and represent them in the text structure and style of an information text. An awareness of the characteristics of both text types is therefore necessary. It is also necessary to consider the purpose and audience for the transformed text.

A possible procedure might involve:

- selecting two text types which possess similar elements, e.g. a narrative and a newspaper article;

- providing a plan for the newspaper article;

- making notes according to the elements of the newspaper article plan e.g. who, when, where, what, why;

- expanding notes into sentences using the formal, third person language of a newspaper report;

- using imagination to complete the transformation, e.g. selecting a source – *The victim of the break-in said today...*

Three-level Guides

What is it?

Three-level guides consist of a series of statements based on information found in text. The statements are divided into levels of comprehension.

- Level One statements require readers to locate relevant information directly from the text. The wording of the statements may not always be exactly the same as in the text but the meaning is similar. This requires a literal level comprehension. Literal level comprehension has been referred to as *reading on the lines*, *right there* and *the author said it* comprehension.

- Level Two statements require readers to reflect on literal information and see relationships between statements. They require children to think and search for answers. This is inferential level comprehension. Inferential level comprehension has been described as *reading between the lines, think and search*, and *the author meant it* comprehension.

- Level Three statements require readers to apply and evaluate information by relating it to their own background knowledge. This is evaluative level comprehension. Evaluative comprehension is often called *reading beyond the lines, on my own* or *the author would agree with it* comprehension.

Why use it?

A three-level guide ensures that pupils reflect on the material they have read, first at the literal, then at the interpretive, and finally at the applied and evaluative level. This means that pupils are guided to use facts to form meaningful concepts as they:

- identify the most important literal details and concepts (Level One)

- interpret relationships between these literal statements (Level Two)

- apply and evaluate this information so that deeper understandings or new ideas evolve (Level Three).

How do you use it?

The three-level guide requires consistent modelling and shared use at a class and group level before pupils are able to use it independently.

Begin by determining the content objectives of the reading. The statements at all three levels must be aimed at these objectives. This is what gives direction and purpose to the guide. Where the content is being drawn from other curriculum areas, these content objectives can be found in the National Curriculum.

Write the applied/evaluative level statements first (Level Three). These should be based on the content objectives and the main idea(s), major concepts and generalisations beyond the text. Write literal level statements next (Level One). These should include information on which the applied/evaluative level statements are based. Finally, write interpretive level statements (Level Two). These should help pupils draw inferences from the information in the text. Include a number of incorrect statements at each level.

The following example takes its content objectives from the National Curriculum for Geography at Key Stage 2:

In investigating how environments change, pupils should be taught:

a   how people affect the environment, e.g. by quarrying, building reservoirs, building motorways;

b   how and why people seek to manage and sustain their environment, e.g. by combatting river pollution, by organic farming, conserving areas of beautiful landscape or of scientific value.

The three-level guide is based on *Viewpoints on Waste* by Rodney Martin (Magic Bean, *In-fact* series).

Level 1: Literal
Tick the statements that say what the author actually said.

_____ 1   The expense of waste disposal is a problem.

_____ 2   People throw away approximately 30kg of household waste every year.

_____ 3   One way to reduce waste is to refuse to buy goods that have unnecessary packaging.

_____ 4   Lots of kitchen and garden waste can be recycled.

Level 2: Interpretive
Tick the statements that you think the author meant.

_____ 1   We buy and use too many disposable things.

_____ 2   We need to find special ways for dealing with toxic waste.

_____ 3   Industries are being creative in finding uses for recycled materials.

_____ 4   Recycling is a government and industry responsibility.

Level 3: Evaluative
Tick the statements that you think the author would agree with.

_____ 1   The disposal of waste is affecting our environment more than ever before.

_____ 2   Every piece of waste ultimately has an impact on humans and other living things.

_____ 3   Ways in which we can prevent waste disposal problems are limited.

_____ 4   People can lessen the waste problem by changing their habits.

Like the reading guide, the three-level guide takes time to produce. However, it must be remembered that it only needs to be done once, and by sharing the workload teachers can benefit from the work of others. Information texts used on a regular basis could have a three-level guide to accompany them.

After Writing Strategies

Editing and Proof Reading

Revising, editing and proof reading are three vital overlapping skills which develop a piece of writing from a crude train of thought scribbled down on paper to a tight clear manuscript ready for publication. Revising generally refers to changes made to the ideas at paragraph level, editing involves clarifying meaning at the sentence level and proof reading is a final check of punctuation and spelling. Children usually understand proof reading, as it involves tangible elements like capital letters, commas and full stops.

Establishing a respect for the value of editing is somewhat harder and may involve regular sentence manipulation for the result to be appreciated as an improvement of the work. While young writers justifiably can't be expected to show a great deal of interest in the revision of a piece of writing, the teaching of all three skills is paramount to the child's ability to manipulate punctuation and grammar for useful means.

Ways to encourage editing and proof reading include:

- demonstrating techniques in regular modelled reading sessions

- using conferences to impart skills

- modelling positive questioning methods for peer or group conferences

- recommending that children read their work aloud to hear mistakes

- modelling the acceptance of adding, deleting and altering as a messy, but necessary, part of revision

- recognising that many readers need to leave a draft for some time to be able to look at it from a new perspective

- limiting early revision experiences to short, easy pieces of writing

- concentrating on only one or two skills at a time

- being aware that most young children learn to revise in the sequence: add, cut and reorder

- supplying helpful editors' checklists

- encouraging the use of computer word processing packages.

Passages for editing and proof reading

When considering texts to be used for demonstrating editing and proof reading, the following factors should be kept in mind.

- Any child's work should only be used with the child's permission; nevertheless, commentary about the work should focus on the positive aspects first and assume the tone of a constructive peer conference, relying primarily on guiding questions and respecting the author's ownership.

- Passages produced by the teacher to highlight a teaching point should be economical in terms of clarifying a focus, but should have a connection to an authentic language context.

- Children relate well to a piece of writing by an author of similar development because they can empathise with the struggles and similarities of the writing process.

Oral editing

Many children can hear pauses in their own reading as indicators of full stops and soon become aware of how their intonation might signal an exclamation mark or comma. One procedure for oral editing is as follows.

- Choose a child who is reading and writing with confidence, but does not know how to punctuate correctly.

- Ask the child if he or she would like the class to help with putting the capital letters and full stops in the right places.

- Copy the child's piece of writing onto a large piece of paper (or OHP transparency) and display it so that the whole class can see it.

- Use this enlarged copy to model the proof reading strategy you want the children to eventually use by themselves.

- The teacher reads the writing, stopping at the end of each sentence.

- The class claps when the teacher's voice stops.

- The child puts in the full stop while the rest of the class observes.

- The teacher points out that the next word after a full stop is a new sentence and therefore must begin with a capital letter.

- The child changes the letter to a capital while the class watches.

- Leave the enlarged text pinned up so that the children can refer to it and even practise the strategy with a partner.

This evolves into a child-owned technique and becomes more powerful as this occurs. If a child has no interest in the purpose, form or audience of a piece of writing, no amount of revising, editing or proof reading will improve it.

| *Publishing* |

What is it?

Publishing is the process of preparing a text for presentation to an audience. There is a myriad of ways in which a text can be published. Publication is important for the way that presentation can enhance the meaning of a text.

Why use it?

Pupils need to develop a growing awareness of how publishing styles have an impact on readers. Layout, illustrations, colour, page size, print size and many other factors have an impact on how a text is interpreted. Pupils will benefit from discussions about how, for example, using all upper case letters can create emphasis, or how ellipses (...) can be used to create suspense.

How do you use it?

As children approach the publishing stage of their writing process, it is helpful to look at and discuss texts that have been written and designed to achieve a similar purpose for a similar audience. For example, a pupil who has written a draft for a picture book might be shown how many pages a picture book normally has, how much print is on each page, how big the pictures are, and how the words and the illustrations combine to create meaning.

A possible procedure might involve:

- selecting texts that achieve a similar purpose for a similar audience
- discussing the presentation features
- reflect upon why these techniques were used
- discuss which of the techniques would be suitable for use in the current context
- publishing.

Strategies for Teaching Information Texts

Teachers can use the following chart to help them identify the skills and knowledge they wish their pupils to develop (see horizontal axis). They can then scan the vertical axis to determine which activities they would like to implement. The dots indicate activities for before, during and after reading that relate to each area.

Activities	Before reading				During reading				After reading			
	to activate and organise background knowledge	to link existing knowledge to new information	to recognise and clarify purpose for reading	to gain an overview of the content	to use context clues to work out difficult vocabulary	to understand the relationship between main idea and supporting detail	to encourage monitoring of comprehension	to identify important information	to use syntactic, semantic and graphophonic cues to identify words	to represent main ideas in another form	to recognise different levels of comprehension	to substantiate information from within the text or by reference
Graphic Organiser	●	●										
Before and After Chart	●	●	●									
Skim Sheets				●								
Anticipation Guide	●	●	●									
Difficult Words Chart					●							
Main Idea Pyramid						●						
Reading Guide					●		●	●				●
Cloze Procedure					●		●		●			
Transforming										●	●	●
Three-level Guide											●	●

Activities	Before writing			During writing			After writing		
	to become aware of text structure	to become aware of language features	to prepare thoughts and notes for a first draft	to vary sentence length and sentence structure	to recall and record significant information	to organise and summarise information in a clear and concise manner	to review text for inaccuracies	to adjust text to suit purpose and audience	to present text in a way appropriate to purpose and audience
Text Reconstruction	●	●							
Text Completion	●	●							
Oral Presentation	●	●	●						●
Drawing	●	●	●						
Direct Modelling	●	●							
Brainstorming			●						
Sentence Manipulation				●		●			
Note-making	●	●	●		●	●			
Editing and Proofreading							●	●	
Publishing									●

Independent Research Projects

The Inquiry Process

Today's world has been coined the Information Age. People are living in societies that generate a greater volume of information than ever before, and this information is processed and stored in a growing number of ways. The development of complex, technological societies is creating greater literacy demands on those who live in them. It is critical that pupils have strategies to identify their informational needs, access the necessary information, and use the information to solve problems in their lives.

Independent projects have often been used as a vehicle to teach children research skills. A six-step inquiry process is outlined here to provide a guide for teachers, pupils and parents involved in the development of these skills. The following guidelines on pages 126 and 127 provide a process that can be used to teach research skills in a motivating, purposeful and supportive context. Each step of the process should be briefly checked by the teacher and/or the parent to ensure understanding and focus. The process assumes the ability to refine thinking, find resources, access resources, make notes, write drafts from notes, revise, edit and publish. The teacher must teach these skills and support pupils as they attempt them.

Identify and Define the Topic

Select a topic on the basis of:

- A problem to be solved, e.g. we are helping my elderly aunt put plants in her garden. She is worried that they might grow too high, be poisonous or send their roots under the paving. We need to identify suitable plants.
- A school problem to be solved, e.g. how can we reduce the likelihood of theft and vandalism at our school?
- An area of personal interest
- Preparation for a public event, e.g. the opening of the Millennium Dome.

Be clear about your purpose. Consider purpose, form and audience.

Develop the topic by brainstorming all that is already known about the topic onto an explosion chart or concept map. This may become a more ordered Structured Overview now or later.

Identify and define keywords. Write up to three focus questions using the keywords. Think what it is it you really want to know. Predict some of the answers. 'How many planets are there in the solar system?' is a closed question. It has a single, one-word answer. 'Why are some planets more likely to have life than others?' is an open-ended question. Open-ended questions are more worthwhile research questions than closed questions.

Consider how the final product will be published and presented. Consider possible forms:

- oral
- written (recount, report, explanation, instructions, persuasive text, letters, faxes, e-mails)
- graphic
- dramatic.

And possible media:
- video
- overheads
- artwork
- software.

Stop! Show your concept map, focus questions and publication/presentation ideas to a parent or teacher.

Locate Resources
List all the possible sources of information. Consider:

- Oral discussions with friends, experts, companies and Government bodies
- Radio programmes
- Books about the topic (personally-owned, school-owned, borrowed, library, bookshop)

- Reference materials such as encyclopaedias, dictionaries and atlases
- Television shows or documentaries
- Videos
- Internet searches
- CD ROMs and software
- Newspapers, journals and magazines.

Use the focus questions and underlined keywords to direct the search for information. Use a search strategy appropriate to each source. Maintain a list of all references used.

Stop! Show your list of resources and search strategies to a parent or teacher.

Select and Record Information
Use skimming and scanning techniques to analyse information for:
- readability
- relevance
- accuracy
- user-friendliness
- fact or opinion
- appropriateness.

Make notes and categorise them according to the focus question they refer to, and the part of the question they refer to.

Stop! Show your notes to a parent or teacher.

Process and Organise Information
Use your notes to draft paragraphs that answer the focus questions. Consider what text type structure might be used. Consider using illustrations, diagrams, tables and charts, and the chosen publication and presentation formats.

Stop! Show your draft to a parent or teacher.

Revise, Edit and Proofread the Project
Read the focus question(s) and check whether the draft answers the questions clearly, comprehensively and concisely. Ask a friend to read it.

Make the changes to ideas, project structure, sentences, words and grammar and punctuation that will enhance the impact of the project. Rehearse the presentation method.

Stop! Show your changes to a parent or teacher.

Present the Project
Present the project to the audience.

Gather feedback on how effective the project was in answering the focus questions.

Stop! Ask your parent or teacher for their opinion of the success of your project.

| Lesson Plans | This sequence of two Literacy Hour lesson plans demonstrates the use of just a few of the strategies suggested in this text. Termly objectives are recorded by initials, year, term and objective number; for example, TL 5.1.26 indicates Text Level, Year 5, Term 1, Objective 26. |

| *Year 5, Term 1, Day 1* | **Objectives**
TL 5.1.21: to identify the features of recounted texts such as sports reports, diaries, police reports, including: |

  - introduction to orientate reader;

  - chronological sequence;

  - supporting illustrations;

  - degree of formality adopted;

  - use of connectives, e.g. *first… next… once.*

TL 5.1.26: to make notes for different purposes, e.g. noting key points as a record of what has been read, listing cues for a talk, and to build on these notes in their own writing or speaking.

Shared Reading *15 minutes*
Text: *Cousteau: An Unauthorized Biography* by K.Comber (Heinemann, 1991)

  - Pre-reading motivation and discussion: brainstorm what is known about Jacques Cousteau (one idea per card).

  - Ask: if the text to be read is a biography of Cousteau, how will this information be arranged? (Chronologically.)

  - Organise the ideas chronologically; discuss information that might be grouped together, e.g. place of birth and reason for fame might be together in the introduction.

  - Read the first three chapters of *Cousteau: An Unauthorized Biography*.

  - Confirm or reject predictions about the order and organisation of information.

Shared Writing *10 minutes*
  - Model the note-making process outlined on page 114 using a page from an encyclopaedia and other sources.

  - Organise information on cards, and group cards according to common criteria and chronological order.

Group Tasks *25 minutes*	
Group A **Pupils and teacher working together**	**Group B** **Word Level & Sentence Level** **Pupils working independently**
<ul><li>Children work on step 5 of the note-making procedure (selecting from a complete text).</li><li>Ask pupils to choose one question from a list designed to be answered within the selected text, e.g. *Why is this person famous?*</li><li>Provide the pupils with a text about famous people and model how, using an example question as a starting point, a reader could use the contents page, index, chapter headings, sub-headings and topic sentences to find the information required in the text.</li><li>Ask pupils to follow the demonstration, locate the information and select the key words necessary to answer the question.</li><li>Ask pupils to use the key words to write a sentence or two that answers the question.</li></ul>	<ul><li>Pupils work on step 3 of the note-making procedure (simple text).</li><li>Ask pupils to read aloud a simple descriptive paragraph about a famous person (teacher-selected).</li><li>Ask pupils to select four or five key words from the paragraph that would help them recall its main idea. Pupils have a copy of the paragraph so key words can be circled, underlined or highlighted.</li><li>Share the key words selected and discuss their worth by debating the merits of those open to contention. Begin by finding the key words common to most individuals or groups. Where words serve a similar purpose, the pupils judge which word carries more meaning. For example, *Jillian has the key word* many *to accompany the key word* attempts. *Alison has the word* four *to accompany the word* attempts. *Which word tells us more about this person's efforts?*</li><li>Ask pupils to use the key words to write a sentence about the paragraph.</li></ul>

Whole-class Sharing *10 minutes*
Children from each group share the process they followed to take notes, highlighting the easiest and the hardest parts of the activity.

Assessment
- Were children able to identify some features of an information text? What do they need to revise?
- Were children able to use meaning, grammatical knowledge and visual cues to identify words and reconstruct sentences?

Year 5, Term 1, Day 2	**Objectives** TL 5.1.21: to identify the features of recounted texts such as sports reports, diaries, police reports, including: ● introduction to orientate reader; ● chronological sequence; ● supporting illustrations; ● degree of formality adopted; ● use of connectives, e.g. *first... next... once* TL 5.1.26: to make notes for different purposes, e.g. noting key points as a record of what has been read, listing cues for a talk, and to build on these notes in their own writing or speaking.

Shared Reading *15 minutes*
Text: *Cousteau: An Unauthorized Biography* by K.Comber (Heinemann, 1991)

● Use copies of text chapters.

● Have each child read a chapter aloud.

● Reconstruct the text as a class.

● Discuss the cues (words and phrases that mark time) used to reconstruct the text.

Shared Writing *10 minutes*
● With permission, use sentences written by pupils in yesterday's lesson (supervised group).

● Model how to organise information on cards and group cards according to common criteria and chronological order.

● Demonstrate how markers of time (e.g. *After leaving home*, Charles Darwin joined...) alert readers to developments in the subject's life.

Group Tasks *25 minutes*	
Group A **Pupils and teacher working together**	**Small Groups** **Pupils working independently**
• Children who worked on step 3 of the note-making process (simple text) continue to make notes. • Pupils work in pairs and use notes on cards to write sentences for a cohesive paragraph.	• Pupils add sentences to the information previously gathered. • Pupils arrange sentences into at least two paragraphs using markers of time to sequence them.

Whole-class Sharing *10 minutes*
Children read their paragraphs to peers from the alternative group. Listeners are to provide one piece of positive feedback, and ask one content question.

Assessment
Make brief notes or complete a checklist to indicate pupils' respective abilities to make notes.

GLOSSARY

active voice – the subject of the verb carries out some action, e.g. *The child drew a picture*

adjectival clause – a clause used to describe a noun or pronoun, e.g. The man *who was carrying an umbrella,* walked past my house

adjectival phrase – a phrase used to describe a noun or pronoun, e.g. The boy *with long legs* won the race

adjective – a word used to describe a noun or pronoun, e.g. He was a *fat* cat

adverb – a word that modifies or more clearly defines the action of a verb, e.g. The boy ran *quickly*

adverbial clause – a clause which modifies or more clearly defines the action of a verb, e.g. The boy ran quickly, *thinking he would miss the train*

adverbial phrase – a phrase which modifies or more clearly defines the action of a verb, e.g. 'The boy ran quickly, *his bag in his hand ...*'

affix – a word used to describe both prefixes and suffixes

alliteration – the repetition of initial sounds in successive words, e.g. *The wind whistled wildly*

anecdotes – a report or description of an observed behaviour

annotation – textual comment in a book which may be written in a margin

apostrophes – a punctuation mark to indicate a *contraction* or *possession.*
contraction: The apostrophe replaces omitted letter or letters, e.g. *hadn't.*
possession: applied to all single or collective noun possessives (except *its*) – the apostrophe is added before the s which indicates ownership: e.g. *John's book; the cat's tail.* For a plural marked by an s, the apostrophe is added after the s: e.g. *cats' tails; girls' hats.*

article – a grammatical marker linked to a noun; may be definite *(the);* or indefinite *(a* and *an)*

assessment – gathering data to better understand the skills, knowledge and behaviours of a learner

auditory texts – text that is heard read aloud

blends – the sounds of two or more letters joined with minimal changes in those sounds, e.g. *st* in *stick*

characterisation – how an author presents a character in speech, action or reaction from other characters

choral reading – the synchronised reading aloud of a common text by two or more people

clause – a group of words within a sentence containing a subject and a verb, e.g. The man *who was wearing a hat,* boarded the train

cloze procedure – instructional strategy involving the completion of incomplete sentences, phrases or clauses

colon – punctuation mark denoting a long pause when speaking, used before a list or to begin a further explanation

compound word – a word as a single unit of meaning but consisting of two separate words, e.g. *buttonhole, football*

concepts of print – recognition that print needs to be arranged in an orderly fashion for effective communication

conjunction – a connecting word, joining words, phrases, clauses and sentences, e.g. *because, and, but, however*

consonant – all letters of the alphabet except *a,e,i,o,u*

context – the cultural or social situation in which language occurs. This may be verbal or non-verbal language

contextual cues – information which comes from both the text, and the reader's interpretation of the text, that helps identify a word or group of words

contextualisation – keeping literacy in the broad linguistic, social and psychological experience of the learner so that response to text is possible

continua – more than one continuum

continuum – a systematic, continuously structured table of identified skills, behaviours and understandings which increase in complexity

contraction – a word which represents a shortened version of one or two other words. Letters are omitted and substituted with an apostrophe, e.g. *did not* becomes *didn't*

conventions of print – rules that govern the customary use of print in literacy

criteria – principles taken as standards of judgment

critical literacy – analysis of the values and beliefs conveyed in a text

cueing systems – any of the various sources of information that may help a reader comprehend a text, e.g. using semantic, syntactic and graphophonic knowledge, pictures, diagrams, background knowledge

cumulative rhyme – a rhyme with many details repeated until it reaches a climax

deconstruction – dismantling a text section by section, to reveal its structure and linguistic features

developmental – changes in the complexity and organisation of behaviour related to growth over time

diagnostic tools – instruments for the assessment of skills, knowledge and behaviours of a learner

dialogue – conversation between two or more people

digraphs – two letters that together represent one sound, e.g. *ch, ck, ai*

Directed Reading Activities (DRA) – step-by-step instruction involving clearly defined purposes for reading and directed questions

directionality – the orientation of English print from left to right and top to bottom

drafting – writing in a rough form. It may be edited later for publication

editing – clarifying meaning at the sentence level

element – a component part, e.g. in literacy: *reading and writing*

embedded – set in a context that makes sense to the reader

evaluative – a level of comprehension involving judgement beyond the text based on background knowledge brought to the text

explanation – form of text which makes facts or situations known in detail

exposition – forms of argumentative or persuasive text

fiction – imaginative narrative in any form

figurative language – language enriched by figures of speech and images created by words, e.g. *The ghostly trees bent close to the ground*

fluency – the ability to read or write language smoothly, easily or readily

form – structure of particular genre

grammar – fundamental pattern of a dialect. The way words are combined to make meaning

graphic organisers (concept maps) – structures or tables that enable a reader to visualise, record and retrieve information from a text

graphophonic – sound-symbol relationship often called 'phonics'

guided reading – a small group, directed reading activity in which the teacher guides comprehension of the text

homonym – a word with the same oral or written form as another, but with different meanings, e.g. *bear (animal); bear (tolerate)*

homophone – a word which sounds the same as another, but which is spelt differently, e.g. *stare, stair*

implicit – a meaning, intended, but not directly stated by an author

indicator – evidence, from gathered data, of acquired skills, knowledge or behaviours used to direct teaching

inferential – a level of comprehension related to understanding implied in the text but not directly stated

inflectional endings – an ending which, when added to a word, changes its form but not the class of word, e.g. *stop, stopped; dress, dresses*

informational text – see non-fiction texts

interactive – communication either between two or more persons or persons interacting with media, e.g. *book, computer*

interjection – exclamation sometimes formed by actual words or sounds indicating emotional noises, e.g. *Oh! Phew! Gosh!*

intonation pattern – vocal pitch that contributes to the meaning of spoken phrases, e.g. *Shut the door. SHUT THE DOOR! Shut the door? SHUT THE DOOR!!* Intonation is used to convey meaning, e.g. sarcasm, questioning, humour

learning journey – personally presenting a report of the products of learning, reflecting skills, knowledge and understanding acquired in that learning, e.g. *taking a visitor on a learning journey around the classroom*

linguistic feature – a language feature of a text type which makes it recognisable, e.g. *grammatical patterns, layout* and *style*

literal meaning – meaning clearly stated in text or in speech

logograph – an orthographic symbol that represents one or more words, e.g. *a pictograph; a symbol ☎ for telephone*

medial vowel – referring to the middle vowel used in a word, e.g. *'u' in cup*

metaphor – an expression in which one idea is described in terms of another, e.g. *the road was a ribbon of moonlight*

miscue analysis – a formal examination of oral reading using running records as a basis for analysing language skills of pupils

mnemonic – technique to assist with remembering something, e.g. *an invented sentence using initial letters of each word to remember a sequence of facts, such as notes on a keyboard* or *a verse to assist in remembering correct spelling such as 'The principal is my pal.'*

modelled writing – teaching the writing process by example and 'thinking out aloud'

modelling – serving as an example of a learner by 'thinking out aloud' and reflecting on learning processes

monitor – to continue to observe learning behaviours, skills, knowledge and understanding

morpheme – the smallest meaningful unit of a word, e.g. *'un', 'reason'* and *'able'* in the word *'unreasonable'*

morphology – the study of the structure of words

narrative – a story expressed orally or in writing

nominalisation – a process is turned into a thing, e.g. *It was announced today that we won the competition* becomes *Our winning of the competition was announced today*

non-fiction – text designed to explain or describe rather than entertain – *see also* **informational text**

noun – a name of a person, place, object, emotion etc.

onset – as in 'onset and rime': the part of a syllable before the 'nucleus': usually any consonants which precede the vowel, e.g. *'tr'* in *'trick'*

orientation – usually the beginning passage of a text. Providing the reader with enough background information to comprehend the text from the writer's perspective

outcomes – effectiveness of a plan or teaching or learning

paragraph – begins with a new line. Used to organise thoughts. A section of a piece of writing used to change focus of time, place or speaker

participle – parts of a verb. Participles help form the tenses of the verb

passive voice – a sentence in which the subject of the verb receives an action instead of carrying it out, e.g. *The man was hit by the car*

personification – a figure or speech giving 'human-like' qualities to animals, ideas, things, e.g. *The moon smiled down upon us*

phase – a stage of development

phoneme – the smallest unit of sound in a word, e.g. *'b'* as in *'book'*

phonemic awareness – the awareness of the sounds or phonemes that make up spoken words

phonic awareness (see also **graphophonic**) – an awareness of the sound-symbol relationship used in words

phonics – a way of teaching which stresses sound-symbol relationships

phonological awareness – the awareness of the sounds that make up words in learning to read or spell

phrase – a small group of words, which is not a complete sentence because it has no verb

plural – a word which represents more than one, e.g. *trees, roses, sheep, women*

portfolio – a collection of pupil's work to evaluate learning progress

predicate – what is said about the subject in a sentence

prefix – part of a word which is the small addition of one or more letters at the beginning of a base word, e.g. *un* in *unhappy*

prepositions – words which show the relationship of one thing to another, e.g. The boy chased his dog *under* the barn

procedure – form of text conveying how to do something

pronoun – a word which stands instead of a noun, e.g. The boy looked for his dog because *it* had run away

proof reading – final check of punctuation and spelling

punctuation – graphic marks used to help readers clarify meaning of written text

recount – a form of text which tells an event in detail

reflection – the process of consciously thinking over acquired skills, knowledge and understanding

report (as a noun) – form of text which is an official or formal account of something

report (as a verb) – presenting an account of something to another

revision – changes made to ideas at the whole text and paragraph level

rime – as in onset and rime: a vowel and any following consonants of a syllable, e.g. *ick* in the word *trick*

root – the meaningful bases of words, e.g. *'aqua'* in *'aquatic'* meaning *water*

rote learning – acquiring new knowledge through repetitive drill

rubric – a scoring device which explicitly states criteria on which judgements are made about quality, understanding and demonstrated proficiency

scaffolding – the provision of structured support which enables pupils to focus on a specific objective by removing the need to deal with peripheral features

scanning – quickly reading material to locate a specific detail such as a name, date or place

segmentation of words – breaking down the components of a word into phonemes, e.g. *ch-ur-ch; c-a-t*

semi-colon – a punctuation mark which joins two parts of a sentence or separates sentence parts in a list, e.g. *The bicycle was broken; its wheel was twisted*

sentence – *simple* – a sentence with one clause, *e.g. Sam hit me*

  compound – a sentence made up of simple sentences joined by conjuctions, *e.g. Sam hit me but I didn't cry*

  complex – a sentence containing a main clause and a subordinate clause, e.g. *I didn't cry when Sam hit me because I wanted to be brave*

semantic cue – information from the meaning of a text or root word, that aids in the identification of an unknown word

shared reading – an instructional strategy where the teacher involves a group of children in text reading for the purpose of modelling reading behaviours

shared writing – an instructional strategy where the teacher involves a group of children in the writing of a text for the purpose of modelling writing behaviours

sight vocabulary – words which are automatically identified

signal phrases – phrases which indicate relationships between parts of sentences. These may include time order, cause and effect, comparison or extra information, e.g. *in the meantime, because of this*

simile – a simile compares two things, referring to a likeness between them, e.g. *He was shaking like a leaf.* Words which are commonly used in a simile are: *as, like, as though, as if etc.*

skimming – reading quickly to gain a general impression of the main idea of a text

sociogram – diagrammatical representation of the relationships between characters

standard English – the accepted form of language for education, government and business

stereotype – a perception based on culturally dominant ideas

strategy – a method employed to improve or modify performance of a task

subject – the subject is a noun or a pronoun of which the sentence is all about

sub-vocalises – moves lips and mouth during silent reading

suffix – a word part added to the end of a base word that changes the meaning of the word, e.g. *en* in the word *oxen*

syllabification – the division of words into syllables, e.g. *won/der/ful*

syntactic cue – knowledge of the grammar and sentence patterns of language used when reading

syntax – the study of how sentences are formed and the pattern and structure of word order and grammar

teaching emphasis – a planning focus or goal for teaching

tense – used to show the time at which the action of a verb takes place, e.g. present tense: *stay*, past tense: *stayed*, future tense: *will stay*

text – spoken or written linguistic communication

text form – also known as **text type** – a category of text with particular structural and language features, e.g. *narrative, limerick, argument, report*

text innovation – the practice of making changes to text

topic sentence – a lead sentence containing the main idea of a paragraph

Venn diagram – overlapping circles that demonstrate elements of subsets that are unique to the subset or common to both

verb – a word which defines an action or a state of being, e.g. *run, walk, imagine, become, sing*

vocabulary – words of language used by a person or group

word derivation – using an affix to change a base word, e.g. *predict – prediction; sign – signature*

working memory (sometimes called **M space**) – the number of discrete elements that the mind can cope with at one time

zone of proximal development (as defined by **Vygotsky**) – the distance between a learner's actual development and potential development through problem solving and support

BIBLIOGRAPHY

ADAMS M. 1990, *Beginning to Read: Thinking and Learning About Print,* 'A Bradford Book', The MIT Press, Cambridge, Massachusetts.

APPLEBEE A.N. 1978, *The Child's Concept of Story, University of Chicago Press,* Chicago.

BARRATT-PUGH C. and ROHL M., *Learning to Read and Write,* Allen and Unwin, Sydney, Australia (in press).

BEAN W and BOUFFLER C. 1986, *Spell by Writing,* Primary English Teaching Association (PETA), Rozelle, NSW, Australia.

BOLTON F. and SNOWBALL D. 1985, *Springboards,* Nelson, Melbourne, Australia.

BRICE-HEATH S. 1983, *Ways With Words: Language, Life and Work in Communities and Classrooms,* Cambridge University Press, Cambridge.

BROCKHOFF V. 1995, Learning Journeys, *Practically Primary,* Volume 1, pp6-11. Australian Literacy Educators Association (ALEA), Victoria, Australia.

BROWN H. and CAMBOURNE B. 1987, *Read and Retell,* Thomas Nelson, Melbourne.

BROWNE H. and MATHIE V. 1990, *Inside Whole Language: A Classroom View,* Primary English Teaching Association, Sydney, Australia.

BRUINSMA R. 1990, 'Learning to ride a bike and learning to read: Children's Conception of Reading', *The Australian Journal of Reading,* Volume 13, No2.

BRUNER J. 1986, *Actual Minds, Possible Worlds,* Harvard University Press, Massachusetts.

BURNES D. and PAGE G. 1985, *Insights and Strategies for Teaching Reading,* Harcourt Brace Jovanovich Group, Sydney, Australia.

BUTLER A. and TURNBILL J. 1984, *Towards a Reading, Writing Classroom,* Primary English Teaching Association (PETA), Rozelle, NSW, Australia.

CAMBOURNE B. 1988, *The Whole Story,* Ashton Scholastic, Aukland, New Zealand.

CASE R. 1985, *Intellectual Development, Birth to Adulthood,* Academic Press Inc. London.

CHALL J. 1984, *Stages of Reading Development,* McGraw Hill, New York, USA.

CHAMBERS A. 1993, *Tell Me – Children reading and talk,* Thimble Press, Gloucester.

CHRISTIE F. and ROTHERY J. 1989, *Writing in Schools, Reader,* Deakin University Press, Geelong, VIC, Australia.

CLAY M. 1987, 'Implementing Reading Recovery: Systematic Adaptations to an Education Innovation', *New Zealand Journal of Educational Studies* 22 (1).

COLLERSON J. 1988, *Writing for Life,* Primary English Teaching Association (PETA), Rozelle, NSW, Australia.

COWLEY J. 1989, *Jim's Trumpet,* Rigby Education, Perth, Western Australia.

CUMMINS J. 1984, *Bilingualism and Special Education, Issues in Assessment and Pedagogy, Multilingual Matters,* Clevedon, Avon.

CUTTING B. 1990, *Talk Your Way To Reading,* Shortland Publications Limited, New Zealand.

DAVEY B. 1983, '"Think Aloud" – Modelling the cognitive processes of reading comprehension'. *Journal of Reading,* 27 (1).

DEREWIANKA B. 1990, *Exploring How Texts Work,* Primary English Teaching Association (PETA), Rozelle, NSW, Australia.

DONALDSON M. 1978, *Children's Minds,* William Collins, Glasgow.

DUFFY G., ROEHLE L. AND MASON J. 1984, *Comprehension Instruction: Perspectives and Suggestions,* Longman, New York.

ECT 418 Language Studies, Children's Writing 1984, *Children's Writing: Study Guide,* Deakin University Press, Geelong, VIC, Australia.

ERICSON L. AND FRASER JULIEBO M. 1998, *The Phonological Awareness Handbook for Kindergarten and Primary Teachers,* International Reading Association, Delaware, USA.

FOUNTAS I. AND PINNELL G.S. 1996, *Guided Reading – Good First Teaching For All Children,* Heinemann, Portsmith, New Hampshire.

FRANK M. 1979, *If you're trying to teach kids to write, you've just gotta have this book,* Incentive Publications, Nashville, Tennessee, USA.

FREEMAN Y.S. AND D.E. 1998, *ESL/EFL Teaching: Principles for Success,* Heinemann, Portsmith, New Hampshire.

FURNISS, E. AND GREEN P. 1991, *The Literacy Agenda,* Eleanor Curtin Publishing, Melbourne, Australia.

GENTRY J.R. 1981, 'Learning To Spell Developmentally', *The Reading Teacher,* vol.34, no. 4, International Reading Association, Newark Delaware, USA.

GENTRY J.R. 1982, 'Spelling Genius at Work: An Analysis of Developmental Spelling in GYNS AT WRK', *The Reading Teacher,* vol 36, no. 2, International Reading Association, Newark Delaware, USA.

GENTRY J.R. 1987, *Spel...is a Four Letter Word,* Ashton Scholastic, Gosford, NSW, Australia.

GOLDSMITH P. AND ROBINSON R. (n.d.), *Developing Word Knowledge* (Pen Note 58), Primary English Teaching Association, Rozelle, NSW, Australia.

GRAVES D.H. 1981, *Writing: Teachers and Children at Work,* Heinemann Educational, Melbourne, Australia.

GREG L.W. AND STEINBERG I.R. 1980, *Cognitive Processes in Writing,* Lawrence Earlbaum Association, New Jersey, USA.

GRIEVE R. AND HUGHES M. (eds) 1990, *Understanding Children,* Blackwell, Oxford.

HEENAN J.E. 1986, *Writing Process and Product,* Longman Paul Ltd, Auckland, NZ.

HENDERSON E.H. AND BEERS J.W. 1980, *Developmental and Cognitive Aspects of Learning to Spell,* International Reading Association, Newark, Delaware, USA.

HILL S. AND HILL T. 1990, *The Collaborative Classroom,* Eleanor Curtain Publishing, Melbourne, VIC, Australia.

HILLOCKS, G. 1986, 'Research Written Composition: New directions for teaching', National Conference on Research in English, *ERIC Clearing House on Reading and Communication Skills.* Urbana, Illinois: National Institute of Education. Quoted in Johnson, Terry D.(1988), *Unriddling the World,* pp 22, 24. 1986.

HOLDAWAY D. 1972, *Independence in Reading. A handbook on individualised procedures,* Ashton Scholastic, Auckland, New Zealand.

JENKINS R. (ed.) 1986, *Spelling is Forever,* Australian Reading Association, Carlton South, VIC, Australia.

JOHNSTON T.D. AND LOUIS D.R. 1985, *Literacy Through Literature,* Methuen Australia, Melbourne, Australia.

JOHNSTON T.D. 1988, *Unriddling the World,* Wesley Foundation for Research in Literacy Inc., South Perth, Australia. *(out of print)*

KROLL B.M. AND WELLS G. 1983, *Explorations in the Development of Writing Theory, Research and Practice,* Wiley, Chichester, UK.

LAHEY M. 1988, *Language Disorders and Language Development,* Macmillan, New York.

LARSON R.L. 1975, *Children and Writing in the Elementary School: Theories and Techniques,* Oxford University Press, Oxford, UK.

LEKI I. 1992, *Understanding ESL Writers: A Guide for Teachers,* Boynton Cook Publishers Inc. Portsmith, New Hampshire.

MALLAN K. 1991, *Children as Storytellers,* Primary English Association, Newtown, NSW, Australia.

MANZO A.V. 1969, 'The Re-Quest Procedure', *Journal of Reading,* November 1969.

MARTIN J.R. 1989, 'Technically and Abstraction: Language for Creation of Specialised Knowledge', Paper presented to Language in Education Conference, Macquarie University, NSW, Australia.

MARTIN J.R. AND ROTHERY J. 1988, 'Classification and Framing: Double Dealing in a Pedagogic Discourse', paper presented to Post-World Reading Symposium: Language in Learning, University of Sydney, NSW, Australia.

MARTIN J.R. AND ROTHERY J. 1986, *Exploring and Explaining: Factual Writing in the Primary School,* paper presented to ARA conference, Perth, Australia.

MARTIN J.R. AND ROTHERY JOAN 1986, 'Writing Report Project': *Working Papers in Linguistics No 4,* Linguistics Department, University of Sydney, NSW, Australia.

MASON J. AND AU K. 1986, *Reading Instruction for Today,* Scott, Foresman and Co., Glenview, Illinois, USA.

MCCRACKEN M.A. AND MCCRACKEN R.J. 1979, *Reading, Writing and Language: A Practical Guide for Primary Teachers,* Peguis, Winnipeg, Canada.

MCCRACKEN MAND R. 1989, *Whole Language Themes – Animals – Ideas for Teachers,* Longman Cheshire Pty Limited, Melbourne, Australia.

MOFFAT J. 1965, *College Composition and Communicating,* No 16, 5 December, pp, 243-48. Quoted in Johnson, Terry D. (1988) *Unriddling the World,* p44, 1988.

MORRIS A. AND STEWART-DORE N. *Learning to Learn from Text. Effective Reading in the Content Area,* Addison-Wesley, North Ryde, NSW, Australia.

NEW ZEALAND MINISTRY OF EDUCATION. 1996, *Reading For Life,* Learning Media Limited, Wellington, New Zealand.

PALINCSAR A. 1984, *The Quest for Meaning from Expository Text: A Teacher Guided Journey.* 'Comprehension Instruction: Perspectives and Suggestions'. Duffy G., Roehler L and Mason J. Longman, New York.

PARIS S. 1989, *Reading and Thinking Strategy Kits,* Collamore Educational Publishing, D.C. Heath and Company, Raytheon Inc., Lexington.

PARKES B. 1990, *Stories to Tell Teacher's Book,* Oxford University Press, Melbourne, Australia.

PHINNEY M.Y. 1988, *Reading With the Troubled Reader,* Ashton Scholastic, NSW, Australia.

PERERA K. 1984, *Children's Writing and Reading: Analysing classroom language,* Basil Blackwell, London.

PRESSLEY M. AND HARRIS K.R. 1990, 'What we really know about strategy instruction', *Educational Leadership,* September 1990, pp.31-34.

PUBLICATIONS BRANCH 1984, *Early Literacy Inservice Course,* Education Department of South Australia.

RAPHAEL T. 1982, 'Question Answering Strategies For Children', *The Reading Teacher,* November 1982, pp185-90.

ROLLER C.M. 1998, So ... *What's a Tutor to Do?,* International Reading Association, Delaware, USA.

ROTHERY J. 1984, 'The Development of Genres – Primary to Junior Secondary School' in *Language Studies: Children Writing, Study Guide,* (ed) Deakin University Press.

ROWE C. AND **LOMAS B.** 1985, *Spell for Writing,* Oxford University Press, Melbourne, VIC, Australia.

SLOAN P. AND **LATHAM R.** 1981, *Teaching Reading is ...,* Thomas Nelson, Australia.

SLOAN P. AND **LATHAM R.** 1989, *Teaching Frameworks,* paper presented to ARA Conference, Perth, Australia.

STEWART-DORE N. (ed) 1986, Writing and Reading to Learn, Primary English Teaching Association (PETA) Rozelle, NSW, Australia.

TEMPLE C.A., NATHAN R.G. AND **BURNS N.A.** 1982, *The Beginnings of Writing,* Allyn and Bacon Inc., Boston, Massachusetts, USA.

TIZARD AND **HUGHES** 1984, *Young Children Learning: Talking and thinking at home and school,* Fontana, London.

TOUGH J. 1977, *Talking and Learning: A Guide for Fostering Communication Skills in Nursery and Infant Schools,* Ward Lock Educational for The Schools Council, London.

VYGOTSKY L.S. 1978, *Mind in Society The Development of Higher Psychological Processes,* (eds) Michael Cole, Vera John-Steiner, Sylvia Scribner, Ellen Souberman, Havard University Press, Cambridge, Mass.

WATERS M. AND **MONTGOMERY J.** *Children's Writing Proposals,* Reading Around Series, Australian Reading Association, Melbourne, Australia.

WEAVER C. 1988, *Reading Process and Practice: From socio-psycholinguistics to whole language,* Heinemann Books, Portsmith, New Hampshire USA.

WEAVER C. GILLMEISTER-KRAUSE L. AND **VENTO-ZOGBY G.** 1996, *Creating Support for Effective Literacy Education,* Heinemann, Portsmith, New Hampshire.

WEAVER C. 1996, *Teaching Grammar in Context,* Boynton/Cook Publishers, Portsmith, New Hampshire.

WEEKS B. AND **LEAKER J.** 1991, *Managing Literacy Assessment with Young Learners,* Era Publications, Flinders Park, South Australia.

WELLS C.G. 1986, *The Meaning Makers: Children Learning Language and Using Language to Learn,* Heinemann, Portsmith, New Hampshire.

WELLS C.G. 1987, *'The language experience of five year old children at home and at school',* in Literacy, language and schooling, (ed) J. Cook-Gumperz, Heinemann, Exeter, New Hampshire.

WESTERBY C.E. 1985, 'Learning to talk – talking to learn: Oral-literate language differences', in *Communication skills and Classroom Success: Therapy methodologies for language-learning disabled pupils,* (ed) C.S. Simon, Taylor and Francis, London.

WESTERBY C.E. 1986, 'Learning to talk – talking to learn', in C. Simon, *Communication Skills and Classroom Success: Therapy methodology for language disabled studies,* College Hill Press, San Diego, California.

WILKINSON A., Barnsley G., Hanna P. and Swan M. 1980, *Assessing Language Development,* Oxford University Press, Oxford, UK.

WONG J. AND **AU K.** 1985, 'The Concept-Text-Application Approach: Helping elementary pupils comprehend expository text', *The Reading Teacher,* 38 (7), March 1985.

UK BIBLIOGRAPHY

First Steps was conceived and developed by **Alison Dewsbury** for the Education Department of Western Australia. The project team worked under her direction.

The following people made major contributions to the original *First Steps* materials:

Bruce Shortland Jones of Curtin University of Technology and **Judith Rivalland** of Edith Cowan University both contributed original work and acted as Consultants to the *First Steps* Project.

Glenda Raison, then of the Education Department of Western Australia, constructed and wrote the *Writing Developmental Continuum.*

Judith Rivalland was responsible for the concept development and construction of the *Continua of Forms.* Supporting material was researched and written by **Glenda Raison** in consultation with **Judith Rivalland.**

Diana Rees, Education Department of Western Australia, wrote the *Spelling Continuum* in consultation with **Judith Rivalland.** Diana also wrote the section on *Spelling Journal* in the *Spelling Resource Book.* **Kay Kovalevs** wrote the *Graphophonic and Word Study* component of this book. Material from the *Spelling Room Notes* written by **Judith Rivalland** were included in this publication.

Diana Rees and **Bruce Shortland Jones** wrote the Reading Developmental Continuum. Diana wrote the chapter on *Children with Reading Difficulties.* **Glenda Raison** wrote the section on *Contexts for Reading.* Bruce Shortland Jones wrote the *Reading Comprehension* section. He also edited all the initial publications of *First Steps.*

Jennifer Evans, Education Department of Western Australia, researched, developed and wrote the *Oral Language Developmental Continuum and the Oral Language Continua of Forms.*

Leanne Allen, then Speech Pathologist Consultant for the Education and Health Departments of Western Australia researched, developed and wrote the *Oral Language Resource Book.*

Ross Bindon, Education Department of Western Australia, wrote the *Teaching Grammar* component of the *Writing Resource Book.* **Kay Kovalevs,** Education Department of Western Australia, wrote the *Problem Solving Approach to Teaching Writing* included in the same book.

The **Principal and Staff of Highgate Primary School,** supported by **Anna Sinclair,** Education Department of Western Australia and **Caroline Barratt-Pugh** of Edith Cowan University, Western Australia, were responsible for the components on teaching children for whom English is a second language. **Kay Kovalevs,** then Deputy Principal of Christmas Island District High School, also made invaluable contributions in this area.

Beverly Derewianka, Lecturer in Language Education at the University of Woollongong contributed the section on the features of non-fiction text forms.

Peter Sloan and **Ross Latham,** then of Edith Cowan University, Perth, Western Australia contributed sections on *Teaching Children How To Write Informational Texts.*

Terry D. Johnson, Professor of Education, Faculty of Education, University of Victoria, British Colombia, Canada made many generous contributions to the books.

Glenda Raison revised and reconstructed the *Writing Developmental Continuum* and *Resource Books* that were published by Longman Cheshire in 1994. **Alison Dewsbury** revised and reconstructed the *Spelling and Reading Continua* and *Resource Books* and wrote the introductory section of all the books for the Longman Cheshire edition.

Caroline Barratt-Pugh wrote the section on *Catering for Diversity* and working with children for whom English is a second language.

ACKNOWLEDGEMENTS

BEARD ROGER. (Ed) (1995), Rhyme, Reading and Writing, London, Hodder and Stoughton.

BEARNE EVE. (1995), Greater Expectations: Children Reading and Writing, London Cassell.

BROWN MAUDE AND **WILLIAMS ALEX.** (1995), Eager Readers: A Whole Language Approach to Literacy in the primary school through using big-books, Giant Steps but sole distribution by Madeleine Lindley Ltd. (this book has no ISBN).

BROWNE ANN. (1996), Developing Language and Literacy 3-8, London Paul Chapman Publishing.

CAMPBELL ROBIN. (1995), Reading in the early years handbook, Buckingham, Open University Press.

CARTER RONALD. (1995), Key Words in Language and Literacy, London, Routledge.

CLIPSON-BOYLES SUZI. (1996), Supporting Language and Literacy: A Handbook for Those Who Assist in Early Years Settings, London, David Fulton Publishers.

COLES M. AND **HALL C.** (1999), Children's Reading Choices, London, Routledge.

EDUCATION DEPARTMENT OF WESTERN AUSTRALIA. (1994), First Steps Worldwide Edition (in eight volumes) Melbourne, Rigby Heinemann.

EDWARDS VIV. (1996), Reading in Multilingual Classrooms, Reading, Reading and Language Information Centre.

ELLIS SUE AND **BARRS MYRA.** (Eds.) (1996), The Core Book: A Structured Approach to using Books within the Reading Curriculum, London, Centre for Language in Primary Education (CLPE).

FOUNTAS I.C. AND **PINNELL G.S.** (1966), Guided Reading: Good First Teaching for All Children, Portsmouth NH, Heinemann.

FOUNTAS I.C. AND **PINNELL G.S.** (1998), Word Matters: Teaching Phonics and Spelling in the Reading/Writing Classroom, Portsmouth NH, Heinemann.

GRAHAM JUDITH. (1997), Cracking Good Books: Teaching literature at Key Stage 2, Sheffield, NATE.

GRAHAM JUDITH AND **KELLY ALISON.** (Eds.) (1977), Reading Under Control: Teaching Reading in the Primary School, London, David Fulton, in association with Roehampton Institute.

HALL NIGEL AND **ROBINSON ANNE.** (1995), Exploring Writing and play in the early years, London, David Fulton Publishers.

MARRIOT STUART. (1995), Read On: Using fiction in the primary school, London, Paul Chapman Publishing.

MEEK MARGARET. (1996), Information and Book Learning, Stroud, Thimble Press.

MOORE MAGGIE AND **WADE BARRIE.** (1995), Supporting Readers: School and classroom strategies, London, David Fulton Publishers.

REES FELICITY. (Ed) (1997), The Writing Repertoire. Developing Writing at Key Stage 2, Slough, National Foundation for Educational Research.

SEALEY ALISON. (1996), Learning About Language: Issues for Primary Teachers, Buckingham, Open University Press.

WEINBERGER JO. (1996), Literacy Goes To School: The Parents' Role in Young Children's Literacy Learning, London, Paul Chapman Publishing.

WRAY DAVID AND **LEWIS MAUREEN.** (1997), Extending Literacy children reading and writing non-fiction, London, Routledge.

First Steps NLS Edition titles available are:

A practical introduction to First Steps
Assessment Teaching and Learning
ISBN 435 01441 2

How to assess children's literacy
Literacy Developmental Continuum
ISBN 435 01442 0

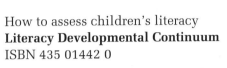

How to assess, plan and teach
Word and Sentence Work at Key Stage 1
ISBN 435 01443 9
Word and Sentence Work at Key Stage 2
ISBN 435 01444 7

How to assess, plan and teach
Shared and Guided Reading and Writing at Key Stage 1
ISBN 435 01445 5
Shared and Guided Reading and Writing at Key Stage 2
ISBN 435 01446 3

How to assess, plan and teach
Fiction and Poetry at Key Stage 1
ISBN 435 01447 1
Fiction and Poetry at Key Stage 2
ISBN 435 01448 X

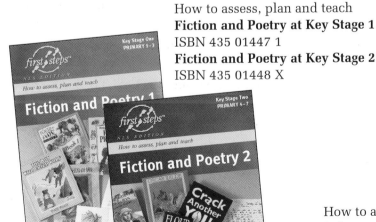

How to assess, plan and teach
Information Texts at Key Stage 1
ISBN 435 01449 8
Information Texts at Key Stage 2
ISBN 435 01450 1

To place your order please phone 01865 888020

FIRST STEPS PROFESSIONAL DEVELOPMENT

Teachers, literacy coordinators, heads, advisors and inspectors have all benefited from *First Steps* professional development courses.

First Steps professional development enables you to:

- Use all the developmental continuum to **assess** the literacy skills and understandings of ALL pupils

- Use this assessment to **select** developmentally appropriate teaching strategies and classroom activities to achieve medium and short term targets

- **Prepare teaching plans** for whole class and differentiated small groups at text, sentence and word level.

To support your literacy teaching further and to gain maximum benefit from your *First Steps* materials, we recommend you attend a *First Steps* professional development course. The *First Steps* books are an integral part of each workshop in the training.

First Steps Tutor Training Course

This five-day training course is suitable for all members of the teaching profession. Tutor training provides a detailed look at the teaching strategies and literacy content of *First Steps.* It prepares participants to present *First Steps* school-based training and to support whole school implementation based on school development plans.

Participants receive comprehensive presenter materials which include session outlines, overhead transparency masters, handouts and audio-visual materials to ensure school based training sessions run smoothly.

First Steps School-Based Training Course

This two-day traing course is suitable for a group of teachers in their own school. School-Based training focuses on *First Steps* approaches and teaching strategies that are the foundation of literacy teaching. The initial two-day course can be extended by the addition of day course options from the full selection of *First Steps* training days.

Contact GHPD on 01865 314630

to find out more about *First Steps*

training courses